Clans and Tartans of Scotland

Clans and Tartans of Scotland

Neil Grant

Lomond Books

Published in 1998 by
Lomond Books
36 West Shore Road
Granton, Edinburgh.
EH5 1QD

ISBN 0 94778 279 6

Printed in Italy

Page 2
A piper in front of Kelvingrove Art Gallery,
Glasgow.

Above
Loch Achray, Ben Venue and the Trossachs
Church.

Contents

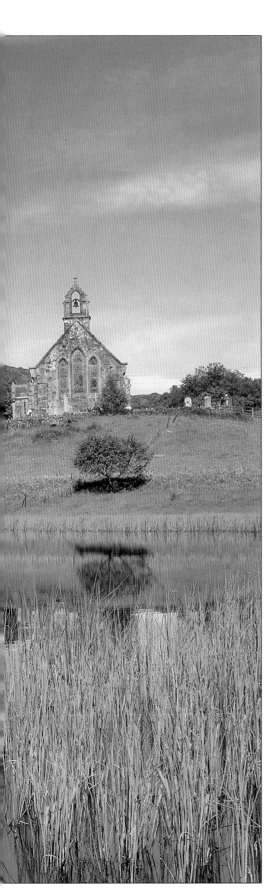

Page 7
Castle Campbell, Dollar, Clackmannanshire.

The Location of the Clans, Battle Sites and Dates

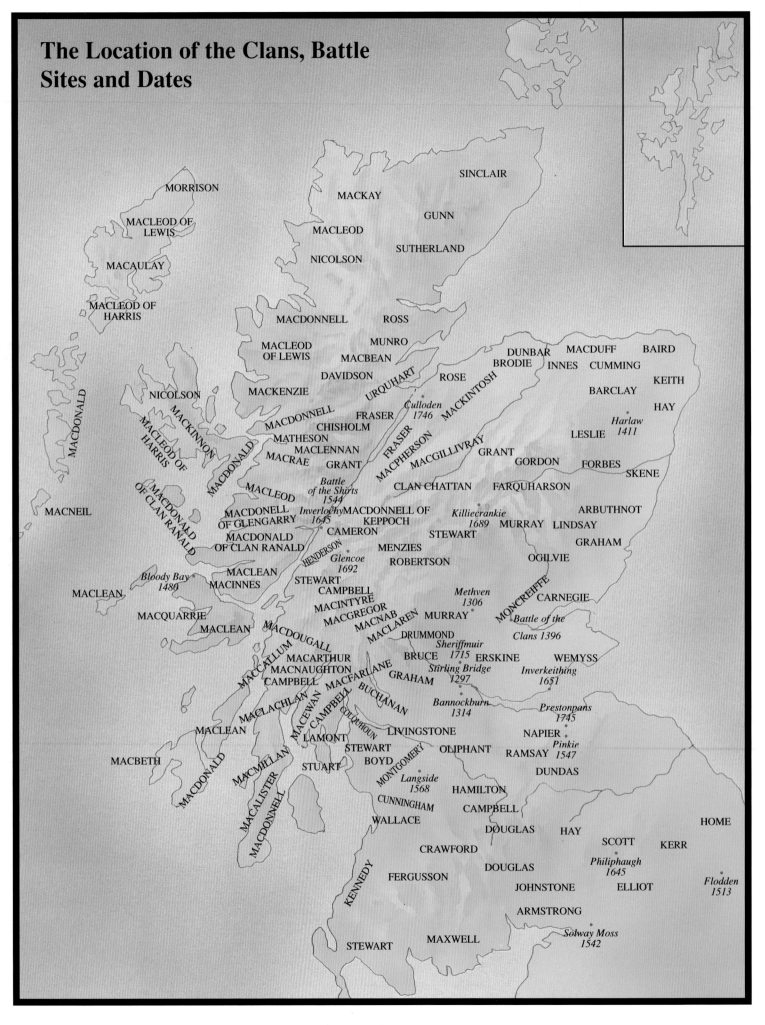

MORRISON

MACLEOD OF LEWIS

MACAULAY

MACLEOD OF HARRIS

SINCLAIR

MACKAY

GUNN

MACLEOD

NICOLSON

SUTHERLAND

MACDONNELL   ROSS

MACLEOD OF LEWIS   MUNRO   DUNBAR   MACDUFF   BAIRD

MACBEAN   BRODIE   INNES   CUMMING

DAVIDSON   URQUHART   ROSE   KEITH

NICOLSON   MACKENZIE   *Culloden 1746*   MACKINTOSH   BARCLAY

MACDONALD

MACKINNON

FRASER   HAY

MACDONNELL   FRASER   *Harlaw 1411*   LESLIE

CHISHOLM   MACPHERSON

MATHESON   MACGILLIVRAY   GRANT

MACLENNAN   GORDON   FORBES

MACRAE   GRANT   SKENE

MACLEOD OF HARRIS

MACLEOD   *Battle of the Shirts 1544*   CLAN CHATTAN   FARQUHARSON

MACDONALD OF CLAN RANALD

MACNEIL   MACDONELL OF GLENGARRY   *Inverlochy 1645*   MACDONNELL OF KEPPOCH   *Killiecrankie 1689*   ARBUTHNOT

CAMERON   MURRAY   LINDSAY

MACDONALD OF CLAN RANALD   STEWART   GRAHAM

HENDERSON   MENZIES

Glencoe 1692   ROBERTSON   OGILVIE

MACLEAN   STEWART

Bloody Bay 1480   MACINNES

MACLEAN   CAMPBELL   *Methven 1306*   MONCREIFFE   CARNEGIE

MACINTYRE

MACQUARRIE   MACGREGOR   MACNAB   MURRAY   *Battle of the Clans 1396*

MACLEAN   MACDOUGALL   MACLAREN

DRUMMOND   *Sheriffmuir 1715*   WEMYSS

MACCALLUM   MACARTHUR   BRUCE   ERSKINE

MACNAUGHTON   *Stirling Bridge 1297*   *Inverkeithing 1651*

CAMPBELL   MACFARLANE   GRAHAM

MACLACHLAN   MACEWAN   BUCHANAN   *Bannockburn 1314*   *Prestonpans 1745*

MACLEAN   CAMPBELL   COLQUHOUN   LIVINGSTONE   NAPIER

LAMONT   STEWART   OLIPHANT   RAMSAY   *Pinkie 1547*

MACBETH   STUART   BOYD   DUNDAS

MACDONALD   MONTGOMERY   *Langside 1568*   HAMILTON

MACMILLAN   CUNNINGHAM   CAMPBELL

MACALISTER   WALLACE   DOUGLAS   HAY   HOME

MACDONNELL   CRAWFORD   SCOTT   KERR

DOUGLAS   *Philiphaugh 1645*

KENNEDY   FERGUSSON   JOHNSTONE   ELLIOT   *Flodden 1513*

ARMSTRONG

STEWART   MAXWELL   *Solway Moss 1542*

6

Introduction

The Scots

About 2,000 years ago, Scots from Northern Ireland began to settle in Argyll, forming the kingdom of Dalriada in about A.D. 500. At that time, the dominant people in Scotland north of the Forth was another Celtic race, the Picts, and for a few years it looked as though Dalriada would be swamped by its more numerous neighbours; but after St. Columba had converted them to Christianity in the late 6th century, the Scots began to expand. The arrival of the Norsemen in the eighth century pushed the Scots farther into Pictish territory, and in 843, Kenneth MacAlpin, King of Scots, gained the Pictish Crown.

Although he is generally regarded as the first king of Scotland, then known as Alba, the kingdom of Kenneth MacAlpin extended no farther south than the Forth-Clyde valleys, and in the north not much farther than the Moray Firth. The task of his successors was to extend the kingdom to its natural boundaries, which they accomplished by the early 11th century.

The reign of Malcolm III (1057-1093), marked the beginning of a new era. Malcolm was English-educated and he married (as his second wife) a princess of both English and Hungarian descent, Margaret. She was one of many prominent English refugees from the Norman Conquest, consequently the English influence was strong and Malcolm moved his capital to Edinburgh, in Anglo-Saxon Lothian.

Of still greater importance for Scotland in general was the influx of Anglo-Norman barons, especially under David I (1124-1153), who, like Malcolm, had spent his early years at the English court and was the premier English baron as well as King of Scots. When he returned to take up the Crown, he was accompanied by many prominent Anglo-Normans whom he endowed with Scottish

estates. From them sprang many future dynasties – Bruce, Fraser, Grant, Sinclair being among many Scottish names of Anglo-Norman origin.

The Highlands

Malcolm III was the last king of Scots to bear a Gaelic nickname – *Ceann Mór*, or Canmore, meaning 'Great Head' – and his reign also marks the growing divide between the Gaelic-speaking Highlands and the largely English-speaking Lowlands. Increasingly divided by language and custom, the Highlands, heavily forested in parts, seemed remote and inaccessible. Malcolm's queen, Margaret, made great efforts to reorganize the Church along Roman lines, but these reforms had little effect

in the Highlands, where the more easy-going customs of the Celtic Church lingered on for centuries.

Feudalism on the Anglo-Norman pattern was soon established in the Lowlands. In the Highlands, its introduction was complicated by the clan system.

It seems obvious that some characteristics of what must be called the clan system (though it was not very systematic) were older than any concept of feudal law. However, it would be wrong to say that the clan system predated the feudal system, or vice versa, and wrong, too, to suppose that feudalism was inimical to the clans. Feudalism and the clan system were established at about the same time and, without feudalism, the clans would not have survived.

In a feudal society, the landlord, who might be the king, allowed a man to hold his land in exchange for services rendered, especially military service. Among the clans of the Highlands, land was held by the chief on behalf of the clan, whose members were, in theory anyway, related to him by blood. Moreover, the chiefship depended to some extent on general consent, though in practice it soon became hereditary. The clan was held together by land no less than by blood.

Conflict over land was common and was aggravated by the lack of legal title. There was a longstanding belief that people had the right to occupy the land on which they lived, but this was not a clearly defined legal principle, and it was more than possible for a clan to lose its land and subsequently its identity to a superior force. Feudalism, however, established land rights. Major clan chiefs, including many of the founders of clans, became vassals of the king, and their landholdings were confirmed by royal charter. Eventually, this strengthened the status of the clans.

Glencoe, site of the battle of 1692 where, on the orders of William of Orange, Campbell forces attacked and slaughtered MacDonalds.

The Clans

The origins of the clans were varied. Some were of Pictish descent, some Norse, and some sprang from the early settlers in Dalriada. The great Clan Donald, a name which in its orginal Gaelic version means 'ruler of the world', was descended from Somerled, a formidable 12th-century chieftain who, notwithstanding his Norse name, could trace his own ancestry to the High Kings of Ireland. He acquired a large dominion in Argyll and the Western Isles, and the various branches of Clan Donald stemmed from his sons. In the east and north, many clan chiefs were descended from feudal Anglo-Norman landlords whose men adopted their names when surnames came into use in the Highlands towards the end of the Middle Ages.

Clan names generally derived from some semi-mythical figure from a much earlier age than that of the historical founder, such as Somerled, who acquired the land that gave them their existence. (As in Ireland, the old Celtic genealogies cannot always be taken on trust, though where they can be checked against other evidence they often turn out to be more reliable than might be expected.) The Campbells are called Clan Diarmaid, after an ancient hero forever lost in the mists of Celtic antiquity, but the Campbell chief (the Duke of Argyll) is called *Mac Cailein Mór*, 'Son of Great Colin', after Sir Colin Campbell, knighted by King Alexander III in1280, a substantial figure whose own ancestors can be traced back, with reasonable confidence, for at least six generations.

Lands were generally built up gradually over time, not only by conquest but by marriage, royal grant or other means. But, whatever the legal title, land had to be held by force, and clan chiefs were therefore eager to acquire men as well as land.

The military aspect of the clan system, combined with devotion to the clan homeland, reinforced the powerful spirit of clanship. Because the men of the clan believed that they and their chief were of the same kin, a much stronger bond existed between chief and clansman than between landlord and feudal tenant. Of course there were social distinctions, but there was also mutual respect and a refreshing lack of lordly superiority or servile

Above
Glen Affric in the Highlands. During the reign of Malcolm III there was a marked divide between the Gaelic-speaking Highlanders and the English-speaking Lowlanders.

Right
Tobermory Harbour, Isle of Mull.
Gaelic culture reached its peak under the MacDonald, Lords of the Isles, who briefly wielded power to rival the King of Scots.

humility from either one. English visitors in the 18th century were surprised to observe that a great clan chief would talk to his herdsmen and labourers on terms of equality.

Clans were numerous and varied. While some prospered and expanded, others declined and disappeared. Large clans developed many branches, septs and dependants, including other, lesser clans that settled on their land. Members did not necessarily even share the same name, and if they did it might have been recently adopted for convenience and, in the event of a change of allegiance, might be changed again. The extent to which they could be regarded as true clans also varied. Some, like the Gordons,

were merely the tenantry of a powerful family, held together by feudal loyalties rather than kinship.

The clan system was essentially a Highland development, but it was also characteristic of the Borders. In both regions, clan loyalties were cemented by constant conflicts, over land, cattle or other objectives, and by the ferocious, long-lasting blood feuds that they provoked. In greater conflicts, such as civil wars, different clans fought on different sides and were motivated as much by clan hatreds as by political or religious animosities. During the Jacobite revolt of 1715, MacLean of Duart addressed his men at Sheriffmuir:

'Gentlemen, this is a day we have long wished to see. Yonder stands Mac Cailean Mór [i.e. Campbell] for King George. Here stands MacLean for King James. God bless MacLean and King James! Gentlemen, charge!'

The Lords of the Isles

Gaelic culture reached its peak under the MacDonald, Lords of the Isles, who briefly wielded power to rival the King of Scots. From Finlaggan on Islay, they controlled a much larger area than their predecessors, the old Norse Kings of the Isles. Although the great chieftains were the Lord's feudal vassals, this was essentially a Gaelic state in which ties of

kinship were dominant, though there was efficient administration of justice through local judges and the Lord's council, and therefore comparatively little of the tribal conflict that scarred the history of the clans.

The power of the lords of the Isles in the early 15th century was demonstrated by Donald, 2nd Lord (and a nephew of the King of Scots). He launched a spectacular assault on the government of the Regent Albany, who had unjustly deprived him of the earldom of Ross. Gathering the western clans, Donald swept across Scotland, meeting the Regent's army in a famous battle at Harlaw, near Aberdeen, in 1411. Casualties were heavy, and neither side could claim a victory, but Donald was forced to withdraw to his own territory.

Ross was subsequently acquired peacefully, but King James I (reigned 1406-1437) and his successors were determined to destroy the Lordship of the Isles. It was a long and bitter contest in which, arguably, the Lords of the Isles brought their final ruin upon themselves, by internal divisions and unprofitable alliances with the English. In 1493 the Lordship of the Isles was officially annexed to the Scottish Crown. John, 4th and last Lord of the Isles, died in a Dundee boarding house a few years later.

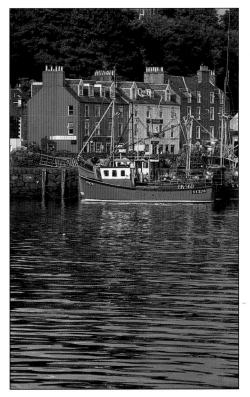

The Stewarts

The royal writ ran fitfully, if at all, in the Highlands. Serious efforts to reconcile the clans were made by James IV (reigned 1488-1513), who wore Highland dress and spoke Gaelic – the last King of Scots to do so. He had some success, and there were many clan chiefs among the dead in the terrible slaughter of Flodden (1513). That victory encouraged the English to renew their attempts to annex Scotland, the Scots being weakened after Flodden by the loss of a large section of the ruling class and – an all-too-common problem – the minority of the monarch. In the Highlands, this was a time of civil wars in the Clan Chattan confederation, of ferocious feuds and barbarous atrocities.

The coming of the Reformation, which made the Lowlands Protestant, had little immediate effect in the Highlands. After the disastrous interlude of Mary, Queen of Scots, another royal minority resulted in more civil wars and Highland feuds. As an adult, James VI coped fairly well with dissident nobles and zealous Presbyterians, but he was relieved when, in 1603, he inherited the English Crown and moved to what he believed would be a more comfortable situation in London.

One of his last acts before leaving Scotland was to proscribe Clan MacGregor, following a massacre of the Colquhouns. This savage reprisal, making the MacGregors outlaws, was a sign of the growing tendency to regard the Highland clans as savage barbarians, best exterminated.

A happier result of the union of the Crowns was the ending of the Border wars. The great raiders – the Armstrongs, Elliots, Johnstones, Kerrs and others – who had conducted their raids and blood feuds for centuries, faded into insignificance.

One way of pacifying the Highlands was to move Lowlanders into the region. For instance, in the reign of James VI, a commercial company in Fife was granted powers in the Isle of Lewis as if it were some New World colony. The 'natives', i.e. the MacLeods, promptly threw them out.

More subtle means were employed in the Statutes of Iona (1609). Officially designed to improve Highland welfare, they aimed in reality at the destruction of the Highland way of life by

undermining the Gaelic language and culture. They were widely ignored, and one unintended and beneficial outcome was to encourage whisky distilling, the result of banning imported spirits.

The efforts of Charles I to impose Anglicanism on the Scottish Church provoked the National Covenant (1638) and the Bishops' Wars, which preceded the civil war in England in which the Presbyterian Covenanters fought on Parliament's side. In the Highlands there was little support for the Covenant, one of its principle supporters being the hated Campbell chief, the Earl of Argyll.

The most spectacular campaign of the civil wars was fought in the Highlands. The Earl of Montrose, himself a former Covenanter, changed sides, partly because he was suspicious of the ambitions of 'King' Campbell. His small force of irregulars, in particular a thousand or so Irish MacDonalds under a brilliant guerrilla leader, Alasdair MacColla, briefly gained control of most of the country until, with MacColla absent, Montrose was defeated by the Scottish army returning from England after the final defeat of the Royalists (1645). A long-term effect of Montrose's activities was to exacerbate animosities between Highlanders and Lowlanders, who became all the more determined to eliminate the threat of Highland raids.

The Scots were shocked by the execution of Charles I (1649), and several Highland clans joined the national rebellion on behalf of his son. It was crushed by Cromwell's highly professional New Model Army, and Charles II escaped abroad. General Monck restored order in the Highlands with Cromwellian efficiency.

The Jacobites

In 1688 the English threw out James II (VII of Scots) to ensure a Protestant monarchy. James had plenty of support in both kingdoms, but squandered it by dithering, and his attempted comeback via Ireland was crushed by William of Orange at the Battle of the Boyne (1690). The Scots who had rebelled on his behalf had won a famous victory at Killiecrankie in 1689 under the dashing Graham of Claverhouse (Viscount Dundee), but he was killed in the battle and the rebellion fizzled out.

The new government promised a free pardon to all Highland chiefs who took an oath of loyalty to the Crown. A minor chief, MacDonald of Glencoe, through no fault of his own, missed the deadline. The result was the Massacre of Glencoe (1692). As Highland massacres went, it was not the bloodiest but, approved by the government and carried out by Campbell troops, it aroused widespread revulsion and intensified the alienation of the Highlands.

During the next half century there were many Jacobite revolts on behalf of James III (the 'Old Pretender'). A significant outbreak followed the Act of Union (1707), which was not generally popular in the Lowlands (and largely ignored in the Highlands). More significant was the 'Fifteen' (i.e. the Jacobite rising of 1715), when the Earl of Mar raised the clans and captured Perth, but then hesitated, giving the government precious time to assemble sufficient forces to deliver a fatal check at Sheriffmuir.

The Highland clans were, of course, not

united. (Had they been, history might have turned out differently.) The commander of the government forces was, after all, the Earl of Argyll, chief of Clan Campbell. The Frasers held Inverness for King George and Whig (pro-Hanoverian) clans – Mackay, Ross, Munro – commanded the north and north-east. Inter-clan hostilities were an inextricable ingredient of the national conflict.

Culloden

The Highland chiefs who rallied to Charles Edward, 'Bonnie Prince Charlie', in the 'Forty-Five' (the Jacobite rising of 1745-1746) were motivated by a sense of loyalty and honour but they, or the wisest of them at any rate, did so with foreboding. In the event, the rebellion came remarkably close to success. The Prince and his predominantly Highland host gained control of

Scotland and advanced into England as far as Derby before discretion, perhaps fatally, overcame valour.

The dreadful end came at Culloden (1746), where the exhausted and outnumbered clansmen were decimated by the troops of the Duke of Cumberland, many of whom, of course, were also Highlanders. 'Butcher' Cumberland took few prisoners, and in the aftermath of the battle a campaign of terror was waged against the clans – and not exclusively Jacobite clans – in a determined attempt to destroy their way of life. Even the wearing of Highland dress was made illegal.

The post-Culloden repression and the Highland Clearances that followed, when Highlanders were dispossessed for the sake of sheep pastures and sporting estates, put an end to the clan system, which had been in slow decline long before Culloden. The new landlords, many of them Lowlanders or Englishmen, introduced other improvements, designed primarily to increase the profits of the estate but, in a few places at least, bringing incidental social benefits. Communications were improved and some new towns built although, on the whole, the Industrial Revolution was little evident in the Highlands.

When Samuel Johnson took his famous tour to the Hebrides with James Boswell in 1773, it was still possible to see a Highland

chief and his clansfolk living in the old way, or at least in what Dr. Johnson assumed was the old way. But time had passed on. Johnson himself, though not much enlightened by his glimpse of an alien culture, was not entirely immune to the myths already gathering in the glens. For the Highlands, long regarded by

southerners as a pit of barbarism, were, now that they had been rendered harmless, assuming a very different aspect. They were coming to be regarded as romantic.

Above
Culloden memorial cairn. The most important event in Scottish history was the Battle of Culloden in 1746 when the Jacobites were defeated. This resulted in the Clanship as the working basis of Highland society being destroyed. Many survivors were later killed by the Duke of Cumberland who authorized the slaying of Jacobites in a form of ethnic cleansing in the name of British Imperialism.

Left
Bonnie Prince Charlie.

Opposite
Loch Lochy and Glen More, the Great Glen, scene of the Battle of Inverlochy in 1645. The clansmen had the amazing ability to march for miles over mountainous terrain in all weathers, fighting with great ferocity. Their weapons were broadswords, axes and bows and arrows.

Killiecrankie Pass, Perthshire, scene of the battle of 1689. John Graham of Claverhouse, 'Bonnie Dundee', led the Jacobites against William of Orange. However, he was shot in the moment of victory, supposedly by a silver bullet.

The Tartans

Tartan was worn in the Highlands during the Middle Ages, though also in other places, such as Renaissance Siena. In early modern times it took the form of the belted plaid, a versatile article in the shape of a rectangle about 5 metres (5½ yards) long, which could serve as cloak, sleeping bag – almost a tent. One situation in which it was not so practical was on horseback, and gentlemen therefore adopted tartan tights, known as trews. The kilt is generally regarded as an 18th-century development, though Gaelic sources suggest it was worn earlier. Tartan was not worn in the Lowlands until after the Act of Union (1707), when some adopted it as a mark of national protest.

Tartan is ancient, but clan tartans are not. There is no solid evidence to indicate that clan tartans existed before the Forty-Five. Some clans may well have worn the same tartan: in the Isles, especially, there was possibly not much choice, and chiefs no doubt sometimes equipped their men with identical plaids for a particular expedition. The local companies that were raised in the Highlands as a kind of police force after the Fifteen were issued with a dark tartan that gave them their name, Black Watch, later passed on to the regiment that replaced them.

The Act forbidding the wearing of Highland dress after the Forty-Five rebellion naturally enhanced its appeal. For defeated clansmen, tartan came to be regarded with nostalgia, and they may sometimes have focused on the tartan once worn by a well-loved

continued. Strictly, a clan tartan should only be worn by those families who have a historic claim to it; but a tartan is not a coat of arms, and Highlanders especially tend to take a relaxed view of the matter. Apart from the new tartans that are still being designed, there are several 'general' tartans, like the Caledonian, which virtually anyone can wear. A rigid attitude would be misplaced since, in the great days of the clans, there were few if any specific clan tartans. Nor had the rules for wearing Highland dress, fairly rigid in principle, yet been devised. In recent years the wearing of tartan has increased, and many who have adopted it for political reasons have discovered that it is a practical and comfortable form of dress.

chief. It was perpetuated by the Highland regiments, formed in large numbers from the shattered clans, and by emigrant clan groups to Nova Scotia and other colonies. By the time the Act was repealed, in 1782, the tartan, no longer everyday wear, had become a potent symbol.

The romanticization of the Highlands, in which the novels of Walter Scott played so great a part, made tartan fashionable. All kinds of people were now eager to claim Highland ancestry, and clan tartans proliferated. Enterprising manufacturers produced new,

ornamental patterns, named after districts, events or persons – there was a 'Wellington' and a 'Waterloo'. The famous visit of George IV to Scotland in 1822 marked the peak of its revival and the King is said to have worn the Royal Stewart tartan, the origin of which is unknown. Later, the Balmoral tartan, sometimes worn by Prince Charles, was designed by Prince Albert and named after Balmoral castle, where Queen Victoria, besotted with the Highlands, even had the curtains made of tartan.

The commercialization of tartan has

Above
Sir Walter Scott, Scotland's most famous writer.

Above left
Preparing to put on a 17th-century kilt. This tartan is Clan Wallace.

Opposite
Murdo MacLean standing next to his loom. He is a weaver of traditional Scottish tweed from Swainbost on the Isle of Lewis.

Balmoral Castle was held for a time by a branch of the Farquharson clan. However, they were Jacobites and lost the estate which was returned to the Gordons. It was later sold to Queen Victoria and was renovated in 1853–55 by Prince Albert. It has been the British Royal Family's Scottish residence ever since.

It is said that tartan is purely a Victorian invention; in fact Queen Victoria extensively decorated Balmoral with tartan furnishings. Others claim that it is of ancient origin, dating from the beginnings of Scottish history.

The Clans and their Tartans

Agnew

MOTTO
Consilio non impetu
By wisdom not by force

*N*o one is precisely sure where the name Agnew originated, though it is thought to derive from the Norman Barony d'Agneaux. Others consider it to be of Celtic origin through the native Ulster sept of O'Gnimh, bards and poets to the great O'Neils of Clan Aodha Bhuidhe in Antrim who later anglicized the name to Agnew.

The fortunes of the family were established in Scotland in 1426 when Andrew of Lochnaw was granted the constableship and lands of Lochnaw Castle. In 1451 he was appointed Sheriff of Wigtown, an hereditary title passed down through generations, and his direct descendents still hold the office today. Other famous Agnews were Sir Patrick, MP for Wigtownshire from 1628 to 1633 and again from 1643 to 1647, having in the meantime being appointed to the baronetcy of Nova Scotia in 1629. The 4th Baronet had a grandchild, Mary Agnew, who married Robert MacQueen, the notorious 'Hanging Judge' of Braxfield. The 5th Baronet married Eleanor Agnew of Lochryan, his kinswoman, and they had 21 children. Sir Andrew was an excellent soldier who commanded the 21st Foot and the Scots Fusiliers at the Battle of Dettingen in 1743. He held Blair Castle in 1746 for the Duke of Atholl against the Young Pretender's forces, led by George Murray, the Duke of Atholl's brother. Murray virtually starved out the garrison but was ordered to return to Inverness to meet the Duke of Cumberland's advances.

Another Andrew married an Irish girl, Martha de Courcy, the daughter of the 26th Lord Kingsale. Unfortunately, he died young leaving the estate to his 16-year-old son to

which the 7th Baronet made great improvements and virtually rebuilt Lochnaw Castle.

Many Agnews emigrated to America where there is still a thriving clan society with its own tartan which was designed by the Chief to unite all Agnews from around the world.

Agnew

Arbuthnott

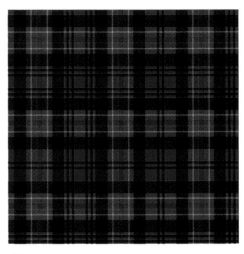

MOTTO
Laus deo
Praise God

*T*he name Arbuthnott derives from a region of ancient lands of similar name in Kincardineshire. Early documentation refers to the name as 'Aberbothenoth' which could be translated as 'mouth of the stream below the noble house'. The lands of Arbuthnott are said to have been aquired by Hugh of the noble family of Swinton through his marriage to the daughter of Osbert Oilfard, known as the 'Crusader'; these events took place during the reign of William of the Lion. In 1282 another Hugh, 'Le Blond', presumably because he had blond hair, became Laird of Arbuthnott. His name appears in a charter of that year as having bestowed land to the monastry of Arbroath to

secure his soul a place in heaven.

In 1355 Phillip de Arbuthnott was the first to be described in a charter as *dominus ejusdem* (of that ilk). His son, yet another Hugh Arbuthnott, was implicated around 1420 in the murder of John Melville of Glenbervie, the vastly unpopular Sheriff of the Mearns. The sheriff was invited to a hunting party with the Lairds of Mathers, Arbuthnott, Pitarrow and Halkerton in the forest of Garvock where he was killed, thrown into a cauldron of boiling water which they had prepared for him. It was claimed that the four conspirators marked the deed by each drinking from the cauldron. The Laird of Arbuthnott was eventually pardoned for his part in the affair and died peacfully in 1446. A direct descendant, Sir Robert Arbuthnott of that ilk, was an adherent to the cause of Charles I, and was elevated to the peerage in 1641 as Viscount Arbuthnott and Baron Inverbervie.

Another important Arbuthnott was Alexander, descended from a junior branch of the chiefly house and a cleric and staunch supporter of the Reformation in Scotland. He was Moderator of the General Assembly of the Church of Scotland which met in Edinburgh in April 1577. Then there was Dr John Arbuthnott, the distinguished physician and political humorist, also claiming kinship to the chiefly family, who went to London to seek his

Arbuthnott

fortune. In 1705, Prince George was taken ill and Arbuthnott was summoned to his sickbed. The prince recovered and Arbuthnott was appointed one of the royal physicians, eventually dying in 1779. The family still resides at Arbuthnott House.

Armstrong

MOTTO
Invictus maneo
I remain unvanquished

The Armstrongs were one of the most formidable of the Border families. A characteristic legend explains how their name derived from a certain Fairbairn, who when the king's horse was killed in a battle, swung his royal master up onto his own horse. In fact, the

Armstrong

Armstrongs may have been of English origin; they are heard of in Cumbria before there is any mention of them north of the border. Their main centre was Liddesdale, extending by the 16th century into Eskdale and Annandale, and a contemporary account says that they could put 3,000 mounted men in the field (certainly an exaggeration). Armstrong heroes, like Kinmont Willie, who made a memorable escape from the English prison in Carlisle, are commemorated in ballad. The most celebrated is Johnnie Armstrong, known as Gilnockie, portrayed as a great smiter of the English. He was the leader of the Armstrongs in the reign of James V, who was determined to suppress the violence in the Borders arising largely out of Armstrong feuds. Gilnockie agreed to meet the King during a royal progress through the Borders, and

appeared with a substantial 'tail' of 40 men. James ordered that they be immediately seized and hanged. Gilnockie's protests having no effect, he remarked: 'I am but a fool to seek grace at a graceless face, but had I known you would have taken me this day I would have lived in the Borders despite King Harry (Henry VIII of England) and you both.' The Armstrongs never recovered from Gilnockie's death and they were dispersed early in the 17th century, much of their land passing into the possession of the Scotts.

Baird

MOTTO
Dominus fecit
The Lord has done this

The name can be traced to a family holding land in Lanarkshire in the 13th century, and a characteristic legend ascribes the family's prosperity to an ancestral feat that saved the life of the king, in this case William the Lion (reigned 1165-1214), threatened by a wild boar killed by Baird's timely spear thrust. The Bairds were later to be found in Banffshire and Aberdeenshire where they filled the hereditary office of sheriff for many generations. Later branches included the Bairds of Newbyth, among them Sir David, a leading soldier of his day who fought in India and in the Napoleonic Wars. Perhaps the most famous descendant of the Bairds was John Logie Baird, the pioneer of television, who was the son of a minister in Dumbartonshire.

Baird

Barclay

MOTTO
Aut agere aut mori
Either to do or to die

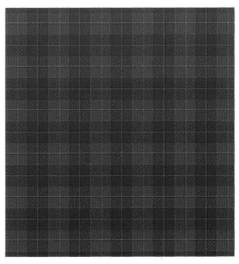

Barclay

The Barclays of Scotland claim to have come to Britain during the Norman Conquest, the name probably originating from the English Berkeley. The founder of the clan is held to be Walter de Berchelai of Gartly, who was Chamberlain of Scotland in the 12th century. Another branch, the Barclays of Mathers, was also descended from an English 'Berkeley', Colonel David Barclay being a leader of the Highlanders who fought for Gustavus Adophus in the Thirty Years' War. He and his descendants became Quakers, and one of them, author of *An Apology for the True Christian Divinity* (1676), was an associate of William Penn, founder of Pennsylvania. The chiefship has been held by the Barclays of Towie since the 15th century. Prince Barclay de Tolly, who commanded Russian forces against Napoleon in 1812, was a descendant of an Aberdeenshire branch of the chiefly family which settled in Russia in the 16th century.

Black Watch

The origin of the Black Watch regiment, historically perhaps the most distinguished in the British army, has been mentioned. The Black Watch tartan is perhaps the oldest indisputably authentic tartan, though no one is certain how the sett and colours came to be decided. There is some similarity to the Campbell tartan, and several early commanders were Campbells; but the Black Watch tartan can hardly have derived from the Campbell, more likely the reverse. Similarly, certain so-called hunting tartans may have been based on the Black Watch. None of these tartans was worn when hunting before the Forty-Five, although Grants sometimes claim that their identical hunting tartan predates the Black Watch. In the early 18th century, the standard dress was the belted plaid, though the kilt (not in the Black Watch tartan) was worn off-duty. By tradition, the pipers of the Black Watch wear the Royal Stewart tartan. They seem to have worn a red tartan from the beginning but we can be certain that, in Hanoverian times, it would not have been the Royal Stewart.

Black Watch

Boyd

MOTTO
Confido
I trust

The name Boyd is said to derive from the Gaelic for Bute, and the name was quite common in Arran and Ayrshire in the late Middle Ages. Sir Robert Boyd was a supporter of Robert Bruce in his campaign against the English and fought at Bannockburn in 1314. The first Lord Boyd became Regent to the young James III in 1465 and was responsible for the King's marriage to a Norwegian princess, which brought the Northern Isles within the Scottish realm. His power made him many enemies, the newly married James turned against him, and he narrowly escaped to England with his life. His son, who had married James's sister and become Earl of Arran, also died abroad, but the line continued through the Regent's second son. The Boyds remained loyal to the Stewarts and were appointed earls of Kilmarnock under Charles I, but lost the title in the Forty-Five. However, one of the 4th Earl's sons became Earl of Erroll by marriage and adopted the disintinguished name of Hay, former holders of the earldom. The current chiefs of both Clan Hay and Clan Boyd are his direct descendants.

Boyd

Brodie

MOTTO
Unite

The family archives were largely destroyed when Brodie Castle at Forres (now maintained by the National Trust for Scotland) was attacked by forces of Montrose during the campaign of 1645. They were a very old family and, although they can no longer be traced with certainty earlier than the 12th century, it is widely agreed that they were of Pictish origin – there are not many families of whom that can be said. The Brodies of Brodie were active in Scottish affairs during the Middle Ages without rising to the highest ranks. Alexander, 11th Chief, was one of the Scottish commissioners who secured the agreement with Charles II in 1649 leading to his coronation as King of Scots over ten years before he was crowned King of England. The 15th Chief, as Lord Lyon King of Arms (the chief Scottish heraldic official), attended the Duke of Cumberland during the Culloden campaign.

Brodie

Below
Corrie Harbour, Arran. Clan Boyd took lands
on the Isle of Arran through the marriage of the
2nd Boyd to James III's sister when he was
created Earl of Arran.

Bruce

MOTTO
Fuimus
We have been

Robert de Brus was a Norman whose castle of Bruis, near Cherbourg, still survives. He came over with William the Conqueror and received extensive lands, mainly in the north of England. His son was one of those Anglo-Norman nobles who associated with the future David I at the English court, and was given Annandale when David succeeded. Later generations married successively a daughter and a niece of William the Lion, thus moving closer to the Crown. The 6th Lord of Annandale was guardian of the young Alexander III and after the death of the infant Maid of Norway, Alexander's only direct descendant, became one of the two chief claimants to the Crown. Edward I of England, as mediator, awarded the prize to Bruce's rival, John Balliol. In the long struggle against English domination, the 8th Robert Bruce established his reputation as Scotland's national hero and ended the English threat by his famous victory at Bannockburn (1314). His successor, David II, was a less inspiring figure who died without an heir. He granted the barony of Clackmannan to a cousin, yet another Robert Bruce, from whom the earls of Elgin, chiefs of Bruce since the 18th century, descended. A kinsman, James Bruce of Kinnaird (1730-1794), became the most famous member of the family in later times through his remarkable travels in Ethiopia.

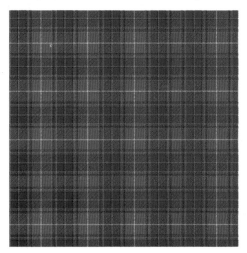

Bruce

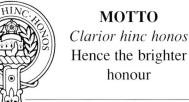

Buchanan

Buchanan

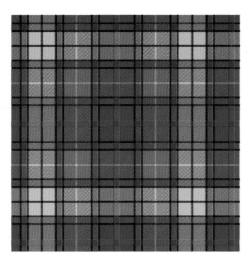

MOTTO
Clarior hinc honos
Hence the brighter honour

Although the Gaelic version means 'seat of the canon', suggesting a priestly origin, the name actually derives from the district east of Loch Lomond, and the lairds of Buchanan owed their land to a vassal of the Earl of Lennox in the 13th century. The name was not adopted until much later, and there were several branches of the clan. William Buchanan of Auchmar, a genealogist who died in 1747, recalled a time when the laird of Buchanan would lay on dinner for 50 men, all living within walking distance, who shared his own name or that of one of the Buchanan septs, which included MacAuslan, MacMillan, MacColman and Spittal. In his own time, the Buchanans were dispersed, and the lands acquired by the Marquess of Montrose. Many settled in Ulster, including the ancestors of James Buchanan (1791-1868), 15th President of the United States. The Buchanans have produced several scholars and poets, including George Buchanan of Killearn (1506-1582), notoriously brutal tutor to James VI and Moderator of the General Assembly of the Scottish (Presbyterian) Church, and Dugald Buchanan (1716-1768), an inspired religious poet whose memorial may be seen at Strathyre, near Callander. The Buchanan lands were sold in 1682 and in 1762, on the death without heir of the 22nd Laird of Buchanan, the chiefship passed to the

Buchanans of Spittal. The island in Loch Lomond where the clan once gathered, now a bird sanctuary, was bequeathed to the Buchanan Society, said to be the oldest clan society in Scotland, in 1939.

Cameron

MOTTO
Aonaibh ri chéile
Unite

The Camerons are one of the greatest Highland clans, but they probably share with the Lowland Camerons a common origin in Fife, the name deriving from Gaelic *cam brun* (crooked hill). Circumstantial evidence strongly suggests a connection with the old MacDuff earls of Fife. How they came to occupy their beautiful and rugged homeland of Lochaber no one knows, but they remained in possession of it, without legal title, for many generations, earning that reputation for courage and ferocity that they reinforced in later times in the British army. The oldest branch is said to be the MacGillonies, who claimed descent from a king of Lorne in the 7th century, though another branch held the chiefship. The first chief of whom there is documentary evidence, traditionally the 11th, was Donald Dubh or 'Black', who led the clan in support of the famous campaign of the lord of the Isles that culminated in the Battle of Harlaw (1411). His younger son became the ancestor of the Camerons of Strone.

Opposite
A statue of Robert the Bruce with the Wallace monument, Stirling. At Scone, in 1306, Robert Bruce was crowned king and began the long campaign to consolidate his title which culminated in the Battle of Bannockburn in 1314.

Overleaf
Loch Ard, Ben Lomond near Loch Lomond where the Buchanan clan once gathered. Nowadays, it is a bird sanctuary.

The lands of the 13th chief were recognized in 1528 as the barony of Lochiel, and the chiefs, a notably distinguished line, have borne the name **Cameron of Lochiel** ever since. They were strong supporters of the Stewart dynasty and Sir Ewen Cameron of Lochiel, the 'Ulysses of the Highlands', was the last Highland chief to hold out against Cromwell in the 1650s. He continued to harass General Monck, the Commonwealth's commander in Scotland, and when Monck decided in favour of the restoration of the monarchy, accompanied him on his march to London. The Camerons were again to the fore in resisting the Protestant succession in 1689 and fought under Graham of Claverhouse ('Bonnie Dundee') at Killiecrankie. Curiously, there were also Camerons fighting as a unit on the other side. They were Lowlanders, raised by a Calvinist shopkeeper in Fife. Lochiel lived until 1719, but was too old to take part in the Fifteen, though his clansmen were again prominent in the Jacobite cause. His grandson, the 19th Cameron of Lochiel, known as 'Gentle Lochiel', may have lacked his grandfather's ferocity, but not his courage. A paragon among Highland chiefs, he was appalled when Prince Charles Edward arrived without French support, or indeed any support, in the Hebrides in 1745. Loyalty triumphed over statesmanship, and when the Cameron pipes were heard approaching Glenfinnan, the Prince knew that the Highlands would rise in his cause. Lochiel, despite two broken legs, survived Culloden and accompanied the Prince back to France, where he died in 1748. Not the least of his achievements was to prevent the retreating Jacobites from sacking Glasgow in 1746, and to this day, when Cameron of Lochiel enters the city, the bells of the churches are rung in his honour.

Of several branches of the clan founded by sons of the first Lochiel, the most famous is **Cameron of Erracht**. Relations with Lochiel were not always amicable, but Donald, 7th Cameron of Erracht, was second-in-command to Lochiel at Glenfinnan. His son Alan emigrated to North America and fought in the American Revolution (1775-1783) before returning to decimated Lochaber, where he unsuccessfully challenged Lochiel for the chiefship. In 1793 he performed a great service for his defeated and dejected clansmen, and for Great Britain, by founding what is now known

Cameron of Lochiel

Cameron

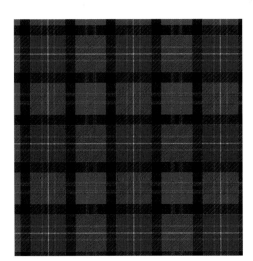

Cameron of Erracht

as the Queen's Own Cameron Highlanders. Tradition says that the regimental tartan was designed by Cameron of Erracht's elderly mother and based on an old Lochaber tartan. It is similar to the MacDonald, but easily recognized by its yellow line.

Glenfinnan Monument, Loch Shiel, Inverness-shire, a round tower topped with a statue of a kilted Highlander, was erected at the spot in 1815 by MacDonald of Glenaladale, whose ancestor's support had been crucial to Prince Charles Edward. However, it was the pipes of the Camerons approaching Glenfinnan which welcomed the unsupported Bonnie Prince Charlie from France, in 1745, confirming that the Highlands would rise to his cause.

Campbell

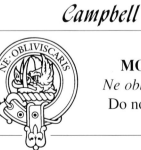

MOTTO
Ne obliviscaris
Do not forget

The Campbells played a major part in local and national affairs from the Middle Ages.

Success breeds enemies, and some of the antipathy to the Campbells, still not completely extinct, derives simply from that. Treachery and atrocities were not confined to them, however, and they were adherents of Bruce and later of the Stewart dynasty until the 17th century. After the glorious Revolution of 1688, they were firm supporters of the government and the chief opponents of the Jacobites in Scotland. The record of the Campbell chiefs, earls and later dukes of Argyll, is hardly equalled by any other family in British history. Though not averse to force, when necessary, the Campbells were adept at expanding their territory by taking advantage of the feuds of their neighbours. As agents of the Government in the West Highlands, they were quick to move in on the lands of defeated rebels, and always endeavoured to secure legal confirmation in the form of royal charters. Among the oldest of clans, they can reasonably be traced back through the 12th-century Lord of Argyll, Somerled, to the Irish High Kings. Their name, originally spelled Cambel, is said to derive from the Gaelic *cam beul* ('crooked mouth'), which fits their reputation for double dealing, but may have been a place name.

The senior branch of Clan Campbell is **Campbell of Argyll**. The chief is known as *Mac Cailein Mór* ('Son of the Great Colin'), i.e. Sir Colin Campbell, knighted by Alexander III in 1280. Staunch support of Bruce, an early example of the Campbell knack of picking the winning side in spite of losing early battles, secured their ascendancy at the expense of their neighbours, the McDougalls. The 1st Earl of Argyll (created 1457) greatly increased his lands by marriage and moved the family seat from Loch Awe to Inveraray on Loch Fyne – a sea loch offering better communications. The collapse of the Lord of the Isles brought more acquisitions, at the expense of the MacDonalds and their allies. The various disturbances of the 16th–18th centuries offered more opportunities, though it was not possible to remain always on the winning side. There were feuds over the chiefship, with Campbells killing Campbells, and the famous Marquess of Argyll, the leading Covenanter and opponent of Montrose during

the civil war, ended under the blade of the Iron Maiden (precursor of the guillotine). His son was also convicted of treason, escaped from Edinburgh Prison, and supported Monmouth's rebellion in 1685, but was captured and executed under the original charge. The accession of William and Mary ended their troubles, and the 10th Earl became a duke in 1701. Of his successors, the most notable was the 8th Duke, a political grandee in Victorian times whose son married one of the Queen's daughters.

Campbell of Breadalbane is the senior cadet branch. The chiefs descended from a son of Lord Campbell (died 1453), and were known as Campbell of Glenorchy before becoming earls and later marquesses of Breadalbane. It was said that at the end of the 19th century Breadalbane could ride 100 miles in a straight line without leaving his property. They had benefited from the proscription of Clan MacGregor in 1603 and on numerous other occasions displayed the Campbell ability to augment their holdings by various, often devious skills, though the 1st Earl (created 1681) was thwarted by the courts after gaining control of the earldom of Caithness through a mixture of craft and brute force. The massacre of Glencoe was perpetrated by the Campbells of Glenlyon, a sept of the Campbells of Breadalbane, but the Earl himself, though blamed by contemporaries, had no prior knowledge of the episode. The line of succession later deviated more than once. One 18th-century earl was a great improver, introducing spinning and building miles of roads, but a 19th-century successor was responsible for devastating evictions of tenants.

The family still holds Glenorchy and certain other properties.

A classic piece of Campbell aggrandisement established the cadet branch, **Campbell of Cawdor** (Calder). The 2nd Earl of Argyll secured the infant heiress, Muriel, first obtaining wardship of her, then – reinforcing law with force – dispatching an armed party to snatch her. She became the bride of his son John in 1510. (Legend relates that in order to prevent the infant heiress being substituted, her mother either branded her with a red-hot key, or her nurse bit off the tip of one finger, or possibly two.) Cawdor Castle (still inhabited by the Campbell Earl of Cawdor), had been built by the father of Muriel. He had a dream that he should set a chest of gold on a donkey and let it wander and build his castle where it stopped. The donkey stopped at a hawthorn tree, and the tree is carefully preserved to this day (cynics may doubt if it is the same tree), growing through a hole in the floor of the keep and up through the roof.

Campbell of Argyll

Campbell of Cawdor

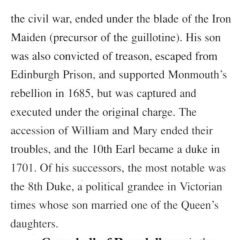

Campbell

Campbell of Breadalbane

Kilchurn Castle situated on the banks of Loch Awe in Argyllshire was founded by Sir Colin Campbell of Glenorchy. The 1st Earl of Argyll (created 1457) greatly increased the Campbell lands by marriage, moving the family seat to Inverarary Castle on Loch Fyne.

The aftermath of Culloden saw the end of the clans as an effective social system, but the Campbells, however, managed to retain much of their ancestral land. Inveraray Castle is still the seat of the Campbell chief.

Carnegie

MOTTO
Dred God

The name derives from estates in Angus, obtained by purchase in the 14th century. Kinnaird, still the seat of the chief, was acquired by marriage a generation or so later by a chief who died at the Battle of Harlaw (1411). The eighth Laird was created Earl of Southesk by Charles II, and the Carnegies remained loyal to the Stewart dynasty, the 5th Earl fighting for James III in the Fifteen and losing his estates as a result. During that campaign, he acted closely with MacDonell of Glengarry, and according to legend this association was responsible for the similarity of the Carnegie and Glengarry tartans. The estates were later regained, again by purchase, and the earldom was restored in 1853. There were several distinguished branches of the family, notably the earls of Ethie (later Northesk), but the most famous Carnegie came from a humbler background. Andrew Carnegie (1835-1919), the great American industrial magnate and philanthropist, was the son of a Dunfermline weaver. He was responsible for many worthy social innovations in his native country, and rebuilt Skibo Castle in Sutherland as his residence.

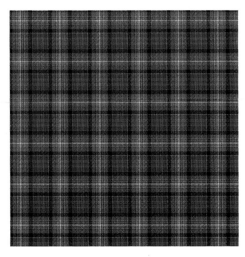

Carnegie

Chisholm

MOTTO
Feros ferio
I am fierce with
the fierce

The Chisholms take their name from a barony near Hawick in the Borders, where there was a Chisholm of that ilk until the end of the 19th century. A 14th-century predecessor became hereditary constable, through his wife, of Urquhart Castle on Loch Ness. He also inherited lands in Moray which, together with his control of the Great Glen, made him a force in the Highlands. Another fortunate marriage in the next generation added Erchless in Strathglas. Its fine tower house later became the seat of the chief (always known as 'the Chisholm', a distinction, one of them remarked, they shared only with the King and the Pope, though in fact other clan chiefs were so addressed). The Chisholms were Catholics, and they fought in the Jacobite risings of the 18th century, though in the Fifteen at least, the Chisholm himself differed from his clansmen and did not take part. That did not stop him from being deprived of his lands, for a time. A son of the chief was killed at Culloden, and three Chisholm brothers were among the 'Seven Men of Glenmoriston' who protected the fugitive prince in a cave. The clan, never numerous, was diminished by emigration and finally dispersed during the Clearances, which, perpetrated by the current chief, signified the death of the clan spirit. Since then, the succession has been diverted far from the original line.

Chisholm

Cochrane

MOTTO
Virtute et labore
By valour and
exertion

The chief of the Cochrane is the Earl of Dundonald, a title created in the early 17th century. The 1st Earl was the son of a man originally named Blair, who married the Cochrane heiress and adopted the family name. Her family was descended from Allan Cochrane of that ilk, who obtained a royal charter from James II for his lands near Paisley, and Allan's presumed ancestors can be traced back in the same place several generations earlier. There was once a Cochrane Castle, or tower house, but no trace of it remains. Nationally, the most famous of recent Cochrane chiefs was the admiral, Lord Cochrane, 10th Earl of Dundonald (1775-1860), who besides notable service for his own country also commanded the naval forces, such as they were, of Chile and Greece during their wars of independence. A great radical and innovator, he provided much of the material for the naval yarns of Captain Marryat.

Cochrane

Opposite
In the 14th century a Chisholm became hereditary Constable of Urquhart Castle on Loch Ness. The appointment was only briefly held by the Urquhart clan.

Colquhoun

MOTTO
Si je puis
If I can

The Colquhoun lands bordering Loch Lomond were obtained by grant from the Earl of Lennox in the reign of Alexander II and were subsequently augmented by useful marriages, one of which added the name Luss, still borne by the chief. It was (and is) an attractive region, and also commanded a major route between Highlands and Lowlands. These circumstances may partly account for the particularly bloody history of the Colquhouns, who were a powerful force in the 15th–16th centuries. Of their many feuds, the worst involved the MacGregors. After one MacGregor assault, the Colquhoun women staged a protest

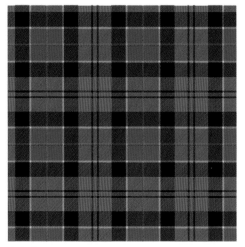

Colquhoun

before King James VI at Stirling Castle, displaying the bloodstained shirts (sheep's blood according to their enemies) of their menfolk slain by the MacGregors. The King granted Colquhoun of Luss a commission of fire and sword against the MacGregors, and his clansmen (800 of them according to one witness) were summoned by the fiery cross. The result was a disaster. They were ambushed by the MacGregors at Glenfruin, 200 were killed, and their cattle and other possessions seized. This was the slaughter that provoked James VI, before departing to claim the English Crown, to proscribe Clan MacGregor. The Colquhouns were never a formidable force thereafter. During the Jacobite rising of 1715, their military enterprise was confined to

preventing the MacGregors from using boats on Loch Lomond. During the 18th century the Colquhouns of Luss became mixed up genealogically with the lairds of Grant, when, following intermarriage, Grants who succeeded to the Colquhoun chiefship changed their name in order to retain the autonomy of the respective clans. The Colquhouns of Luss still live at Rossdhu on Loch Lomond, in a fine villa rather than the old castle, of which only ruins survive.

Crawford

MOTTO
Tutum te robore reddam
I will give you safety by strength

The Crawfords can be traced to a medieval barony in Lanarkshire. Sir Reginald of Crawford was sheriff of Ayr towards the end of the 12th century. His descendant, Sir John (died 1248), had two daughters, one of whom became the ancestor of the Lindsay earls of Crawford, the other the mother of William Wallace, the leader of resistance to the English. His son received Auchinames from Robert Bruce and his descendants held the property until the present century. The Crawfords of Crawfordland and the Crawfords of Kilburnie also traced their descent from Sir John. Thomas, a member of the Kilburnie branch, was associated with Mary, Queen of Scots, whose service he entered in France. He broke with her after the murder of her second husband, Lord Darnley, and in 1571 captured Dumbarton Castle from her adherents with a small band of followers after scaling the defences with ropes and ladders.

Crawford

Cumming (Comyn)

MOTTO
Courage

At a critical time in Scottish history the Comyns were the most powerful family in the land. William Comyn was an Anglo-Norman magnate who came to Scotland with David I. He was made chancellor, but the founder of the clan was his nephew, Richard, who married a granddaughter of Donald Bán, King of Scots (1093-1097). That was the first of a series of advantageous Comyn marriages which, by the late 13th century, gave them possession of three of the 13 Scottish earldoms. In the constitutional crisis that followed the

Cumming (Comyn)

death of the Maid of Norway (1290), the Comyn chief (the Black Comyn) had a claim to the throne, along with John Balliol and Robert Bruce (grandfather of the future king). John Balliol was accepted by both his rivals, and the Black Comyn married Balliol's sister. Their son was the Red Comyn. Subsequently, Balliol rebelled against English domination, Edward I conquered Scotland, and Wallace, the leader of Scottish resistance, was defeated. That left the younger Robert Bruce and the Red Comyn as potential leaders, both having strong claims to the throne. There was no love lost between them, as Balliol had bestowed Bruce's estates on Comyn, and a meeting was arranged in a church, early in 1306. There, Bruce killed Comyn and rapidly had himself annointed king at Scone. Bruce's ultimate success was a disaster for the Comyns, who were ruthlessly dispossessed and destroyed. The only son of the Red Comyn was killed at Bannockburn fighting for the English. One branch, the Cummings of Altyre, north of Badenoch, survived, becoming a considerable force in Moray where they conducted ferocious feuds with Clan Chattan. The 13th chief of Altyre married a daughter of Sir Ludovic Gordon of Gordonstoun. His grandson inherited the title and thereafter the chiefs were known as Gordon-Cumming.

Cunningham

MOTTO
Over fork over

The name, which first occurs in the 12th century, derives from a district in Ayrshire. The Cunninghams of Kilmaurs, near Kilmarnock, expanded their lands by marriage, acquiring Glencairn, and in 1488 became earls of Glencairn. In the disturbances of the 16th century, the 2nd Earl lost the earldom, but it was later restored to his brother. The most famous of his descendants is the 8th Earl, the leader of the Scottish rebellion in favour of Charles II in 1653. In spite of its failure, Glencairn survived until the Restoration (1660), when the grateful Charles II made him Lord Chancellor. The 14th Earl was a friend and patron of Burns, who wrote a lament for him on his death in 1791. He was the last of his line, and the earldom became dormant. The present chief is descended from a younger son of the 3rd Earl. There were many other landholding

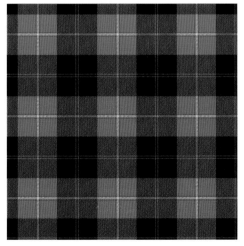

Cunningham

Cunninghams – Auchinarvie, Caprington, Craigend and Robertslane – who descended from sons or cousins of the 1st Earl.

Davidson

MOTTO
Sapienter si sincere
Wisely if sincerely

The Davidsons are said to have ancient links with the Comyns, and after the destruction of the Comyns became a sept of Clan Chattan. They were involved in a long feud with the MacPhersons, among others. In 1370, when the Camerons invaded Clan Chattan territory, Davidson of Invernahaven fell out with Cluny Macpherson over a point of military precedence, with the result that the MacPhersons withdrew and the outnumbered Davidsons were slaughtered. They are also said to have been involved in the famous Battle of the Clans at Perth in 1396, at which King Robert II was a spectator, and the casualties, no doubt to the King's satisfaction, were enormous. For many years the chiefship was held by the Davidsons of Tulloch, who acquired their land north of the Cromarty Firth through marriage.

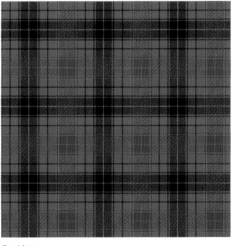

Davidson

Overleaf
The gaunt ruins of Threave Castle was built on an islet in the River Dee. It was a stronghold of the Black Douglases, built by the 3rd Earl of Douglas known as Archibald 'the Grim'.

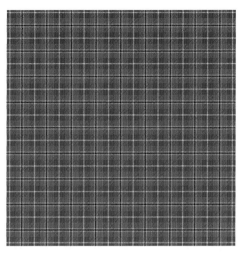

Douglas

Douglas

MOTTO
Jamais arrière
Never behind

The ramifications of the powerful families of Douglas are vast, but they were probably all descended from William of Douglas, who held land south of Lanark in the 12th century. His great-grandson was 'the good Sir James' nicknamed the Black Douglas by the English, who stands with Wallace and Bruce as one of the heroes of the Scottish wars of independence. He commanded the left wing at Bannockburn (1314) and died fighting in Spain while on his way to take the Bruce's heart to the Holy Land. Many of his immediate relations died fighting the English, but his nephew succeeded him and was made Earl of Douglas in 1358. He also gained the earldom of Mar by marriage, and his son George was the 1st Earl of Angus. Meanwhile, the earldom of Douglas passed to Archibald the Grim, a son of the first Black Douglas (additional genealogical confusion is caused by the tendency of these magnates to father sons out of wedlock). From Threaves Castle in Galloway, Archibald ruled the Borders with some efficiency, though he did not, of course, stop the constant raiding. It should be remembered, also, that the authority of the King of Scots was comparatively weak: Douglas wielded more power than the ineffective Robert II. His son, the 4th Earl of Douglas, won a duchy for himself in France, but the power of the Black Douglases in Scotland was waning. After the death of the 5th Earl, his

Earl, his young sons were killed in Edinburgh (1440), but family fortunes were largely restored by the 7th Earl, who was also Earl of Avondale, and the 8th Earl, who regained Galloway. The efforts of King James II to exert his authority led to a meeting at Stirling where Douglas, though under a safe conduct, was fatally stabbed by James personally. His successor, the 9th Earl and last of the Black Douglases, not surprisingly rebelled and was forced to flee to England when the estates were confiscated and the earldom extinguished.

Paradoxically, the Black Douglas was shortly replaced by the Red Douglas, who was Earl of Angus and a direct descendant of the 1st Earl of Douglas. He took part in the suppression of the Black Douglases and was rewarded with some of their estates. His son, the 5th Earl, known as 'Bell-the-Cat', took the lead in hanging some of James III's favourites, an act he described as 'belling the cat' (i.e. as a warning to mice). One of his sons was the poet Gavain Douglas, first to translate Virgil's *Aeneid* into English. In the 1520s, the 6th Earl of Angus was the most powerful man in the kingdom until driven into exile by his many enemies. He had married Queen Margaret Tudor, widow of James IV and sister of Henry VIII of England. Their daughter married Matthew Stewart, Earl of Lennox, and became the mother of Lord Darnley and grandmother of James VI and I. They had no son, and the Angus earldom passed to another branch. The 11th Earl was created Marquess of Douglas, and the 3rd Marquess was raised to a dukedom, but he died childless and his titles passed to the Duke of Hamilton. The chiefship remained with the Douglases who in due course became earls of Home and eventually produced a British prime minister.

There was nearly always a Douglas close to the centre of power. After the Red Douglases came the Douglases of Dalkeith, later earls of Morton. Sir William Douglas, known as the Knight of Liddesdale, was killed by the 1st Earl of Douglas in 1353, but his nephew, Sir James Douglas of Dalkeith, married a daughter of James I and became Earl of Morton in 1458. The 4th Earl was Regent during the minority of James VI and made himself very unpopular so that when James came of age he had him executed.

The house of Douglas of Drumlanrig was descended from a younger son of the 2nd Earl of Douglas, who gave him the barony. His descendants were supporters of the Stewarts in the 17th century and became earls (1633) and dukes (1684) of Queensberry, prominent political figures in Scotland and Great Britain. The 2nd Duke was largely responsible for persuading the Scottish parliament to pass the Act of Union (1707). The 4th Duke, a cousin of his predecessor, was a notable sporting figure in the 18th century, known as 'Old Q'. On his death (1810) the ducal title passed to the Duke of Buccleuch, the marquessate to Sir Charles Douglas of Kelhead, whose descendants included the 8th Marquess, for whom the Queensberry rules of boxing were named. He was the father of Lord Alfred Douglas and nemesis of Oscar Wilde. Another branch of the Douglases, deriving from a younger son of the 1st Marquess of Douglas, became earls of Selkirk in 1646. The 5th Earl of Selkirk is remembered as the founder of Scottish colonies in Canada in the early 19th century.

Drummond

MOTTO
Virtutem coronat honos
Honour crowns virtue
On Compartment
Gang warily

The name derives from Drymen, near the foot of Loch Lomond. Sir Malcolm de Drymen prospered through support for Bruce, gaining land in Perthshire and Stobhall which was acquired through marriage in 1345. Castle Drummond, famous for its gardens, was built by John, Lord Drummond, in the late 15th

Drummond

century. The 4th Lord Drummond was made Earl of Perth in 1605, and commanded a considerable clan, including the Drummonds of Hawthornden which included William (1585–1649), a great literary figure. Under James VII and II, Perth and his brother, the Earl of Melfort, were said to rule Scotland, and they followed the King into exile in 1688, being subsequently raised to dukedoms. The 2nd Duke (or 5th Earl) was a leader of the Jacobites in 1715, and his son commanded the Jacobite left at Culloden. The lands were forfeit, but returned under the General Act of Restoration in 1784. The original Drummond lands later passed through an heiress to another family, but the present Earl of Perth, a descendant of the 3rd Duke's brother, still has his seat at Stobhall.

Dunbar

MOTTO
In promptu
In readiness

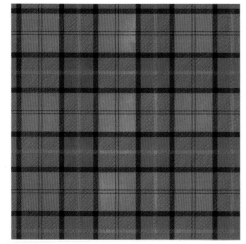
Dunbar

Dunbars were to be found at an early date in many parts of Scotland, but the seat of the earls of Dunbar was Dunbar Castle in Lothian, granted to the former Earl of Northumberland (who had been expelled by William the Conqueror) by Malcolm Ceann Mór, his first cousin. The Dunbars, who had some claim to the throne themselves, were ill-disposed towards Bruce until after Bannockburn, but the Earl signed the Declaration of Arbroath (1320), the Scottish statement of independence. His wife, 'Black Agnes' held Dunbar Castle for several months

against an English siege in 1337. She was Countess of Moray in her own right, and while Dunbar was confiscated by James I, the Dunbars prospered in Moray, where they feuded incessantly with their Innes neighbours. Cadet branches existed as far apart as Caithness and Galloway, where the Dunbars of Mochrum produced several men eminent in Church and State. William Dunbar (died c. 1520), regarded by some as rivalling Burns as Scotland's greatest poet, probably came from Dunbar itself, though his family is obscure.

Elliot (Eliot)

MOTTO
Fortiter et recte
Boldly and rightly

The Elliots were a notorious Borders clan whose territory was in upper Liddesdale, from where they conducted their raids against their neighbours, Scots and English, for centuries. At times the Elliots of Redheugh, the

leading family, held that formidable landmark of the Borders, Hermitage Castle, south of Hawick. The origin of the name is uncertain, and there were probably several. No less than 70 alleged versions of the name are listed in the 17th century. From that time the senior house, which today holds the chieftainship, were the Eliots (different spelling) of Stobs, founded in the 16th century. They were descendants of the Elliots of Redheugh, where the chief has his seat. From a younger son of the 2nd Laird of Stobs descended the family that became earls of

Elliot

Minto, the 1st Earl being a notable Governor-General of India in the early 19th century. His great-grandson, the 4th Earl, followed in his footsteps, becoming Viceroy of India in 1905 despite having, at an earlier age, broken his neck riding in the Grand National.

Opposite
Hermitage Castle was at times the stronghold of the Elliots of Redheugh. The castle dates back to the 14th century and is an impressive sight beside Hermitage Water, north of Liddesdale.

Above
Dunbar Castle in East Lothian was once an imposing fortress and commanded an important position on the south-east coast of Scotland. All that remains are these romantic ruins.

Erskine

MOTTO

Je pense plus
I think more

Erskine is the name of a notable family who were descended from the lords of Erskine, near Renfrew, but who were not, strictly speaking, chiefs of a genuine clan. Their destiny was closely linked with that of the

Erskine

Stewarts. Sir Robert Erskine was Chamberlain of Scotland in the 14th century, and his grandson, the 1st Lord Erskine, claimed the vacant earldom of Mar, an ancient, Pictish title. The title was not confirmed for several generations. Meanwhile, the 5th Lord Erskine was guardian to the young James V, and his son performed the same function for the infant James VI. In gratitude, James's mother, Mary, Queen of Scots, not only confirmed the carldom, but created a new one, presumably to circumvent a future confiscation, so that Lord Erskine became Earl of Mar twice over (the two earldoms later passed to separate heirs). The 1st Earl (in the new creation) was the grandfather of the builder of Braemar Castle on Deeside, who was Lord Treasurer under James VI. His younger sons were the ancestors of the future earls of Rosslyn and earls of Buchan. The 6th Earl of Mar was the somewhat irresolute leader of the Jacobite rising of 1715 and lost the earldom as a result.

Farquharson

MOTTO

Fide et fortitudine
By fidelity and
fortitude

The Farquharsons were a branch of the Shaws and members of Clan Chattan. They took their name from Farquhar, son of a Shaw chief, and their acknowledged founder was Finlay, who died fighting the English at the battle of Pinkie (1547). A Celtic harp, the instrument that preceded the pipes in the Highlands, which is now in the National Museum of Antiquities, is said to have been given to Finlay's widow by Mary, Queen of Scots. His sons and grandsons spawned several cadet branches, most of them holding their land from the Earl of Mar, whose castle at Braemar the Farquharsons later acquired. In the 17th–18th centuries the Farquharsons were robust supporters of the Stewarts, none more so than 'Colonel Anne' during the Forty-Five. She was the daughter of John Farquharson of Invercauld, who had fought in the Fifteen, and her husband, a Mackintosh, was on the Hanoverian side. Another branch of the Farquharsons held Balmoral. They too were Jacobites and lost the estate which returned to the Gordons and was later purchased by Queen Victoria.

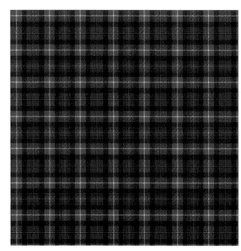

Farquharson

Fergusson

MOTTO

Dulcius ex asperis
Sweeter after
difficulties

The name was broadly distributed in Scotland at an early date, and it would be hard to ascribe all the 'sons of Fergus' to a single ancestor. The most notable family, Fergusson of Kilkerran, north-east of Girvan, was regarded as chief by other Fergussons in the south-west. Baronets from 1703, they included the Scottish historian, Sir James Fergusson, whose brother, Bernard, was a leader of the Chindits in Burma during the Second World War. In general, Fergussons have been more prominent in scholarship than war. The poet Robert Fergusson, who died in 1774 aged 24, influenced Burns, who himself had a monument erected on his grave. A contemporary (though no known relation) was Adam Ferguson, who was a chaplain to the Black Watch (and himself took part in their charge at Fontenoy), before becoming professor of philosophy at Edinburgh University and a friend of Sir Walter Scott.

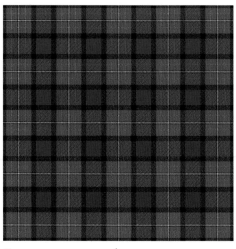

Fergusson

Forbes

MOTTO
Grace me guide

The old county of Aberdeenshire is the home of the Forbes, and the present Lord Forbes retains part of the ancestral estates on Donside. Traditionally, there is a connection with the Urquharts, and possibly the Grants. Sir Alexander Forbes of that ilk married into the royal family and was raised to the peerage in 1445. The Forbes (originally For-beis, two syllables) were neighbours, and for centuries enemies, of the Gordons. It was said that Lord Forbes was able to raise 1,000 men in the 16th century, but the senior line on the whole did not provide strong leadership, and by the 17th century there were several other families, like that of Lord Pitsligo, of equal if not greater status. Among them was the family of the Bishop of Aberdeen and his brother William, 'Danzig Willie'. A prosperous merchant in the Baltic trade in Aberdeen, he was the builder of Craigievar Castle, a magnificent seven-storey tower house now owned by the National Trust for Scotland. Clan Forbes was active in the Jacobite risings of the 18th century, with representatives on both sides. During the Forty-Five, Duncan Forbes of Culloden epitomized the torn loyalties of that conflict. He was practically the only significant representative of the government in the north. A man of honour, good sense and humanity, he failed to ameliorate the ruthless behaviour of Cumberland's forces after the battle which, by ironic coincidence, took place close to his own home. 'That old woman', Cumberland called him.

Forbes

Above
The attractive town of Braemar seen from Creag Choinnich. Braemar Castle, built by the 7th Lord Erskine, was captured by the Farquharsons in 1689 and burned by John Farquharson of Inverey.

45

Fraser

MOTTO
All my hope is in
God

The name is of French origin, and the earliest known Frasers were probably descended from an Angevin named Frezel. The early genealogy is complicated; there is a connection with Keith, that being a district of Lothian where early Frasers held land. Not all Scots called Fraser belonged to the Highland clan, whose Gaelic name is *Mac Simi*, 'son of Simon'. The Simon referred to is supposed to be Sir Simon Fraser who fought with Wallace and Bruce and was executed by the English. His contemporary, and a kinsman of sorts, was Sir Alexander Fraser, chamberlain of Scotland under Bruce and founder of the Frasers of Philorth in Buchan. By marriage, the Frasers of Lovat acquired land in Aberdeenshire but their homeland remained the districts adjoining Loch Ness. They were severely mauled in the Battle of the Shirts, against the MacDonalds, in 1544, but survived and prospered in the 17th century. The most memorable of several Simon Frasers of Lovat was the 11th Lord Lovat, who

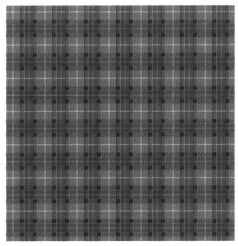

Fraser

Left
Beautiful Craigievar Castle was built by William, 'Danzig Willie' Forbes who was a prosperous merchant in the Baltic trade in Aberdeen. It is a magnificent seven-storey tower house now owned by the National Trust for Scotland.

followed a fascinatingly devious course throughout the Jacobite period and was executed in London – the last peer to be beheaded – after the Forty-Five. Though aged 80 and sick, he conducted a memorable defence at his trial and swapped insults with the crowd on his way to execution. His son later raised the Fraser Highlanders, whose service in Canada partly accounts for the frequency of the name in that country, for example the Simon Fraser University in British Columbia. In the 19th century the chiefship passed to a cadet house, the Frasers of Strichen, who also produced some famous military heroes. The 16th Lord Lovat raised the Lovat Scouts in the Boer War, and the 22nd Chief led British commandos landing in Normandy on D-Day, allegedly wearing a white polo-neck sweater and preceded by his piper.

Gordon

MOTTO
Bydand
(Remaining)

Gordon

The Gordons dominated much of north-east Scotland for a long period. They were not strictly a clan, more a collection of loosely related feudal lords sharing the same name and (an advantage in the power struggle) holding their land by royal charters. Genealogists have distinguished some 150 main branches, but it is likely that they were all related to Sir Adam of Gordon who, belatedly but effectively, supported Bruce against the English and was

rewarded with land in Strathbogie. The name appears to derive from a district in Berwickshire, and Sir Adam's forefathers were possibly Anglo-Norman. The family prospered in the 14th century, largely due to marriage, and acquired the earldom of Huntly. Like the Campbells in the west, the Gordons were agents of the early Stewart kings in their efforts to control, or subdue, the Highlands, and their position offered plenty of opportunity to build up their own empire in the north-east. The numerous vacancies caused by the slaughter at Flodden (1513) brought them the earldom of Sutherland, with its vast estates, and in 1599 the Earl of Huntly became a marquess. Private wars continued against the Grants, Mackintoshes, Stewarts of Moray and others and, following the takeover of Strathnaver from the Mackays, an unsuccessful assault was made on the earldom of Caithness. But the power of 'the Cock o' the North' was in decline in the 17th century, and the 2nd Marquess was executed by the Covenanters in 1649. The dukedom of Gordon was created for the 4th Marquess by Charles II. It later passed to the Duke of Richmond, who inherited the Huntly estates, and the marquessate passed to the Earl of Aboyne, a direct descendant of the 1st Marquess. The chiefship remained with his descendants, whose seat is Aboyne Castle. Of other Gordon castles, Huntly itself is now a picturesque ruin, and little more remains of Gordon Castle, the Bog o' Gight, former residence of the marquesses of Huntly.

A different kind of residence, Haddo House, is a magnificent Robert Adam house in Aberdeen, named for perhaps the most distinguished of other Gordon dynasties. Gordon of Haddo fought on the royalist side during the 17th-century civil wars and was imprisoned in 'Haddo's Hole' in St. Giles, Edinburgh, before being executed. The property was restored after the Restoration of 1660, and Sir George Gordon of Haddo was created Earl of Aberdeen. The 4th Earl was British prime minister at the time of the Crimean War.

Opposite
An evocative image of pipers playing outside Stirling Castle. Sir Patrick Graham of Dundaff was Keeper of Stirling Castle and died fighting the English in 1297.

Graham

MOTTO
Ne oublie
Do not forget

The name comes from an English manor whose proprietor, William de Graham ('Grey home'), acquired Abercorn and Dalkeith under David I in the 12th century. His

Graham

descendants inherited land in the Highlands. The Grahams have an unsurpassed record of militant nationalism. Sir Patrick Graham of Dundaff, keeper of Stirling Castle, died fighting the English in 1297, and his nephew, known as the 'richt arm' of Wallace, met the same fate in 1298. A later Patrick became Lord Graham in 1445, and the 3rd Lord Graham, who later died at Flodden, became Earl of Montrose. His descendant, the 5th Earl, later Marquess, was the famous, if over-romanticized leader of the Royalist cause in 1644-1645, whose Irish MacDonalds, led by Alasdair MacColla, conducted one of the most spectacular campaigns in British history. The Earl was finally defeated and executed with customary barbarity in 1650, but an equally remarkable general appeared in his distant kinsman, John Graham of Claverhouse, known as 'Bonnie Dundee' (or, to his opponents, 'Bloody Clavers'), who, under Montrose, harried the Covenanters and died winning a great Jacobite victory at Killiecrankie (1689). The 4th Marquess of Montrose became a duke in 1707. The 3rd Duke was largely responsible for securing repeal of the act proscribing Highland

dress in 1782. The ducal seat was originally Buchanan Castle by Loch Lomond, acquired in 1680, and later Mugdock, or Montdieu, Castle in Strathblane. There were numerous substantial branches and sub-branches, some of whom wear a separate tartan, that of **Graham of Menteith**.

Grant

MOTTO
Stand fast

The origin of the name is the French *grand*, but the Grants claim an ancient lineage as members of *Síol Alpin*, the stock of (Kenneth) MacAlpin, and kin to the MacGregors. The chiefs can be traced to hereditary sheriffs of Inverness in the 13th century, one of whom acquired lands in Strathspey, the main Grant homeland. In the 15th century the Grants were established in Strathspey under Grant of Freuchie, later called Castle Grant, and there were others beyond the Great Glen who were more or less independent. The history of Clan Grant is better documented than most, partly due, perhaps, to the absence of major disasters. They had their share of feuds, and suffered frequent raids by MacDonalds and Camerons, but the chief power in the region was the Earl of Huntly and his Gordons, with whom, on the whole, the lairds of Grant remained on amicable

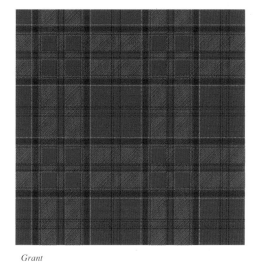

Grant

terms. By the late 16th century relations were less good, but the power of Huntly was beginning to decline, to the Grants' advantage. During the 17th and 18th centuries, they were generally Whiggish in sympathy, though the Grants of Glenmoriston were supporters of the Stewarts. It was impossible to avoid trouble in that era, and during the civil wars Strathspey was attacked by Montrose and the Covenanters successively. In 1688 the Laird of Grant adhered, officially at least, to William of Orange, though many of his clansmen were Jacobites. After the rising of 1715, the Laird of Grant managed to regain Glenmoriston for his Jacobite kinsman, an example of clan solidarity despite ideological differences. The Grants defended Inverness against the Jacobites in the Forty-Five, but without enthusiasm or success, though Sir Ludovick Grant was active in hunting down Jacobites after Culloden. In 1766 Sir James Grant, in his endeavours to prevent the break-up of the clan, founded Grantown-on-Spey, and in 1820, in response to a minor affray known as the Elgin Raid, the Grants were summoned by the fiery cross, the last occasion on which a Highland clan was raised in that

traditional manner. Though Freuchie was a barony, the chiefs of Grant showed no great ambition for further social advancement. When King James VI and I offered to make the 5th Lord of Freuchie Earl of Strathspey, he received the memorable reply: 'And wha'll be Laird of Grant?' In Victorian times, however, the chief became Lord Strathspey in the peerage of the United Kingdom, and subsequently, through an earlier marriage with the Ogilvies, inherited the Scottish earldom of Seafield as well. The titles have since been separated, but the chief remains Lord Strathspey.

Gunn

MOTTO
Aut pax aut bellum
Either peace or war

The name is of Norse origin, and the possible progenitor of the Gunns was a Norse earl of Orkney, who inherited land in Caithness and Sutherland in the late 12th century. Clan Gunn was never large, and was involved in long and bloody feuds with powerful neighbours, particularly the Keiths, and later the Mackays and the Sinclairs. They were largely dispersed during the Clearances in the early 19th century. Some of them moved to the coast and became fishermen in tiny ports where the absence of a harbour meant that the catch had to be landed on the beach. A vivid picture of such communities at the turn of the century appears in the novels of Neil M. Gunn (1891-1973).

Gunn

Hamilton

MOTTO
Through

Hamilton is a famous name in British history, though not, except in a restricted sense, of a Highland clan. A minor Northumbrian lord, Fitzgilbert of Hameldone, who also held land in the Lowlands, profited from his support of Bruce in the wars of independence and acquired the barony of Cadzow, later Hamilton. His 15th-century descendant married the widow of the Master of Boyd, Earl of Arran, the title passing to the Hamiltons. They built Brodick Castle in Arran, now owned by the National Trust for Scotland.

Hamilton

The Boyd widow was also a daughter of King James II, and the Hamiltons were now close to the throne (the 2nd Earl of Arran was Regent to the infant Mary, Queen of Scots), a position that attracted powerful enemies, notably the Stewart earls of Lennox and the Douglas earls of Angus. A notably controversial character was the illegitimate son of the 2nd Earl, Sir James Hamilton of Finnart, responsible for the deaths

Left
The River Spey. In 1766 Sir James Grant, in his endeavours to prevent the break-up of the clan, founded Grantown-on-Spey in Morayshire.

of the then current Earl of Lennox and, to a large extent, of his kinsman Patrick Hamilton, the first Protestant martyr in Scotland. More creditably, he introduced the style of the French Renaissance, which he combined fruitfully with Scottish tradition in the façade of Falkland Palace. In the 17th century the earls of Arran became dukes of Hamilton, but lost the title through their support for Charles I. It passed by marriage to a Douglas. Cadet branches included the dukes of Abercorn, descended from a younger son of the 2nd Earl of Arran, and the earls of Haddington.

Hay

MOTTO
Serva jugum
Keep the yoke

The chief of Clan Hay holds the hereditary title of Lord High Constable, and enjoys precedence over all other hereditary peers in Scotland. The family is of Anglo-Norman origin, and has held the title of Erroll since 1178. According to tradition, their ancestors, descended on the female side from the old Celtic earls of Strathearn, were involved in notable exploits against the Vikings. The 3rd Hay of Erroll, co-Regent of Scotland in the 13th century, married a Comyn, and the 5th acquired Slains, formerly Comyn property,

whose noble ruins grace the coast of Aberdeenshire. The nearest neighbour of note, as James Boswell later remarked, was the King of Denmark. Erroll was elevated to an earldom in 1452, and by that time various cadet branches had acquired considerable estates elsewhere. For many generations, the Hays of Erroll continued to play a prominent part in Scottish affairs. The 9th Earl led the Catholic party after the death of Mary, Queen of Scots, which led to the partial destruction of Slains Castle, but the family survived the difficult times of the 17th century without serious loss. The 13th Earl was briefly imprisoned for his support of the Jacobites in 1715. Under his sister and successor, Mary, Countess of Erroll in her own right, New Slains became a centre for Jacobite resistance. She raised the clan for Prince Charles Edward in 1745, and a kinsman, John Hay, was the Prince's secretary, though by all accounts an ineffective one.

Later earls tended to be men of outstanding physical as well as political stature. The 19th Earl (died 1901) may have owed his physique to his habit of taking a daily bath in sea water pumped up the cliffs at Slains.

Hay

Henderson (Mackendrick)

MOTTO
Sola virtus nobilitat
Virtue alone
ennobles

The Hendersons are said to have lived in Glencoe before the MacIain MacDonalds, whom they served as bodyguards and pipers. There were other groups of Hendersons or Mackendricks (the names are the same in Gaelic), not all connected, as far apart as Caithness (where they formed a sept of Clan Gunn) and the Borders, where they were apparently connected with the Elliots. The leading house was Henderson of Fordell, one of whose branches produced Alexander Henderson of Leuchars, the minister who took a leading role in drawing up the National Covenant in 1638 and was Moderator of the Assembly in Glasgow that reorganized the kirk on Presbyterian lines.

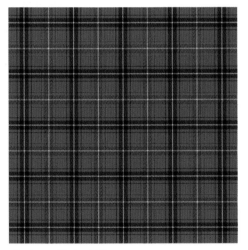

Henderson (Mackendrick)

Home

MOTTO
A Home, A Home,
A Home

The name is pronounced Hume and some Homes, including the philosopher David Hume, changed the spelling of their name to agree with the pronunciation. It derives from a barony in the Borders, and there was an association with the Douglases in the 14th–15th centuries. The 3rd Lord Home, named, like practically all his predecessors and successors, Alexander, was executed by the Regent Albany in 1516 for conspiring with the English to overthrow him. The Homes frequently held the office of Warden of the March, and they probably deserve some of the credit for the fact that the anarchy of the Borders was less pronounced in the east, their territory, than the west. The Homes themselves were split by the Reformation, and the 5th Lord Home lost his estates. They were restored to his son, who became Earl of Home in 1605. The line ended with his son, and the title passed to a fairly distant cousin, a descendant of the 1st Lord Home. The 14th Earl of Home resigned his title to become British prime minister in 1963. He was later created Lord Home of the Hirsel, the family seat.

Home

Innes

MOTTO
Be Traist

It was said that the good fortune attending the chiefs of Innes was due to three factors: there had always been male heirs; no Innes had married an unsatisfactory wife; they were never in debt. The 25th Chief no doubt reflected on this proud record when he inherited the dukedom of Roxburghe in the 19th century. He traced his descent from a Fleming named Berowald, who gained the barony of Innes, on the Moray Firth, by charter of Malcolm IV in 1160. Thanks largely to those well-judged marriages, the chiefs of Innes amassed considerable territory, and branches were established all over the north; but the progress of the line was less smooth than tradition maintained. The 18th Chief was killed in a quarrel with his kinsmen over the chiefship in the 16th century, and a 17th-century successor met his death after being betrayed by his own son. Sir James Innes sold Innes to the Earl of Fife in the 18th century and removed himself to England. The title Earl Innes was created for the 5th (2nd Innes) Duke of Roxburghe in 1836.

Innes

Above
The Three Sisters, Glencoe, Argyllshire. The
Hendersons are said to have lived in Glencoe
before the MacIain MacDonalds, whom they
served as bodyguards and pipers.

Johnstone

MOTTO
Nunquam non paratus
Never unprepared

Johnstone is a common name of territorial origin ('John's tun'), and clearly not all Johnstones were related. The notable Borders clan used to meet in the Devil's Beef Tub, near Moffat, at the head of Annandale, but they were also to be found in neighbouring dales, and became divided into numerous branches. The Johnstones of Annandale often held the office of Warden of the Western Marches, in rivalry with the Maxwells of Nithsdale. Both Johnstone and Maxwell were killed around the end of the 16th century and this, almost the last of the great Border feuds, was ended by royal intervention in 1623. The leading figure in the 17th century was Sir James Johnstone, who became Earl of Hartfell in 1643. His kinsman, Archibald Johnstone of Warriston, was, with Alexander Henderson, author of the National Covenant (1638) and his association with Oliver Cromwell led, fatally, to his exclusion from the general pardon at the Restoration. The line died out in the 18th century and was succeeded by the Johnstones of Westerhall in Dumfriesshire.

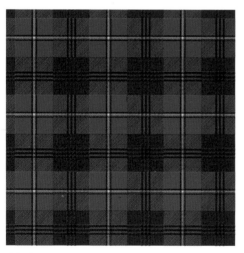

Johnstone

Right:
The Devil's Beef Tub, near Moffat at the head of Annandale, Dumfriesshire was once the meeting place of the Borders Clan Johnstone.
Overleaf:
Culzean Castle built by the Kennedys.

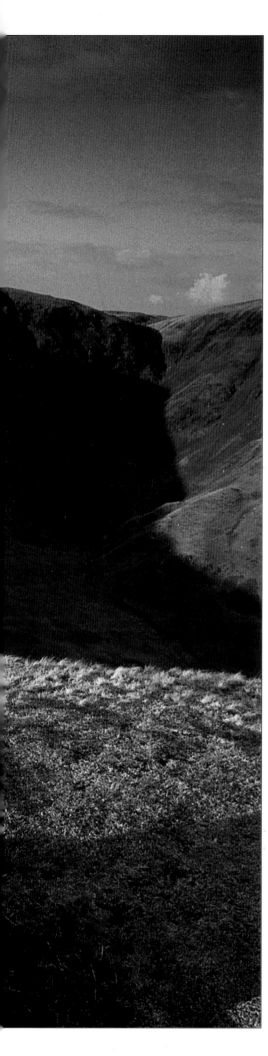

Keith

MOTTO
Veritas vincit
Truth conquers

The Keiths, an ancient Celtic family, held the hereditary title of Marischal, later Earl Marischal of Scotland for about 600 years. They held land in Buchan, and in the 14th century, marriage to the heiress of Ackergill took them to Caithness, where they were involved in a long and relentless feud with Clan Gunn. They became more powerful in the time of Bruce, acquiring land all over the country. By the 16th century it was said that the Earl Marischal could travel from Berwick to John o' Groats, a two-week journey, stopping each night on his own property. Among Keith properties was the Castle of Dunnottar, in a spectacular setting on the east coast south of Stonehaven, where the honours of Scotland were taken for safe keeping during the civil wars of the 17th century. Since the Earl Marischal was obliged to be present at every battle, it is surprising how many of the Keiths survived to a good age. Nor did they confine their campaigning to Britain. A brother of the 9th (and last) Earl Marischal, having fought for the Jacobites in 1715, pursued a successful career on the Continent, eventually dying in 1758 in the service of Frederick the Great, who had a statue of him erected in Dresden.

Keith

Kennedy

MOTTO
Avise la fin
Consider the end

The home of the Kennedys is Carrick in Strathclyde. They appear to be connected with the ancient Celtic Lords of Galloway, and augmented their possessions by marrying useful heiresses, including a daughter of Robert II, which brought them to national prominence. Her son became the 1st Lord Kennedy (1457)

Kennedy

and was one of the regents to the under-age James III. His brother was Bishop of St. Andrews, Chancellor of Scotland, and regarded as a second founder of St. Andrews University. There were also Kennedys in the Highlands, said to be descendants of a fugitive from justice who fled to Lochaber. The 3rd Lord Kennedy was created 1st Earl of Cassillis in 1510 and died at Flodden in 1513. The 2nd Earl was killed by Campbell of Loudon and the 3rd Earl died in suspicious circumstances at Dieppe. His successors held to the Reformed religion, and the 4th Earl, called 'King of Carrick' attempted to assert control of the lands of the abbey of Crossraguel by roasting the Abbot (who was rescued by the Kennedys of Bargany, then feuding with the senior house). The 5th Earl was Lord High Treasurer during the reign of James VI and I. When the 8th Earl died childless, the title passed to the Kennedys of Culzean. They were responsible for the magnificent Culzean Castle, neo-Gothic on the outside, Adam's most elegant neo-classicism on the inside, and now the

Scottish National Trust's most popular property. It was given to the Trust by the 5th Marquess of Ailsa, a title held by the Kennedy chiefs since 1831.

Kerr

MOTTO
Sero sed serio
Late but in earnest

Versions of the name were common in the medieval Borders, and probably came from more than one source. The long rivalry between the two chief houses of the Kerrs was believed to derive from two 14th-century brothers, Ralph, ancestor of the Kerrs (or Kers) of Ferniehirst, and John, ancestor of the Kerrs of Cessford. The two strongholds were only 6 miles (10 km) apart in Teviotdale, and though they sometimes combined against the English, they fought each other with equal ferocity. One or other often held the office of Warden of the Middle March. In the 16th century, Cessford supported the pro-English policy of the Douglases and Ferniehirst that of James V and details of the conflict between them make gruesome reading. The feud was still going strong under Mary, Queen of Scots (Ferniehirst pro-, Cessford anti-), but eventually petered out as peace came to the Borders. In 1631 Anne Kerr of Cessford married William Kerr of Ferniehirst, who thus united the Kerrs under his title of 3rd Earl of Lothian, previously held by the Cessford Kerrs. Their son became a marquess in 1701.

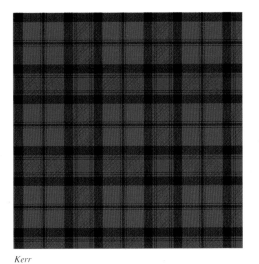

Kerr

Lamont

MOTTO
Ne parcas nec spernas
Neither spare nor dispose

The Lamonts came from Cowal and were probably connected with the original King Comgal (died 537). The clan took its name from Ladman, a grandson of Ferchar, who was a chief in Cowal in the late 12th century, and spread into Argyll. The home of the chiefs was at Inveryne on Loch Fyne until the 15th century, later at Toward Castle. They were never numerous and suffered from the handicap of powerful neighbours, the Campbells. In the civil wars of the 17th century, Sir James Lamont of Inveryne fought reluctantly with the Campbells, though his sympathies were royalist. He was captured by Montrose and, at his suggestion, enthusiastically changed sides, hoping to recoup territory lost in previous generations to the Campbells with the aid of Montrose's MacDonalds. With the defeat of Montrose, the wrath of the Campbells fell on Lamont and, in one of the most atrocious incidents of its kind (they were not few), the clan was massacred. Later chiefs of Lamont maintained a reduced existence at Ardlamont, overlooking the Kyles of Bute, until the property was sold in the 19th century. The Lamonts of Knockdow, not far from Toward Castle, alone retained their ancestral estates, which the 15th Laird left in trust for the clan. A remarkable relic of the Lamonts is the Lamont harp, made about 1450, now in Edinburgh.

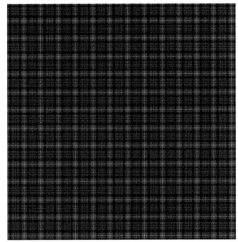

Lamont

Leslie

MOTTO
Grip fast

The name comes from a place in Garioch, north-west of Aberdeen. It is uncertain that all Leslies were related to the early lairds of Leslie. Sir Andrew Leslie was one of the signatories of the Declaration of Arbroath (1320) and his descendants were earls of Rothes from 1457. Later earls played a prominent part in national affairs, especially in the 16th–17th centuries. Alexander 'Sandy' Leslie (died 1661) was descended from the Leslies of Balgonie and, at a further remove, Balquhain, perhaps the most distinguished branch. They were involved in a long feud with the Forbes and later members included John Leslie, Bishop of Ross, a prominent opponent of John Knox during the Scottish Reformation. Sandy Leslie was made Earl of Leven by Charles I in 1641, but commanded the Covenanting army during the civil wars. He retained command of the Scottish army into his seventies, relinquishing it to David Leslie, a grandson of the 5th Earl of Rothes, who defeated Montrose, later resisted Cromwell (unsuccessfully), and became 1st Lord Newark in 1661. A dispute over the succession to the earldom of Leven between the current Earl (later Duke) of Rothes and the Earl of Melville, a grandson of Sandy Leslie's daughter (herself Countess of Leven in her own right), was resolved by the death of Rothes in 1681.

Leslie

Lindsay

MOTTO
Endure fort
Endure boldly

Lindsay

The Lindsays were Lowlanders whose name derived from a district in England. Sir Walter de Lindsay was associated with the future David II, when he was in England, and his successor acquired the lands of Crawford in Clydesdale. The family continued to hold land on both sides of the Border until the wars of independence. Their support of Bruce lost them their English estates, but they acquired more lands, in Angus, and became earls of Crawford in 1398. The 1st Earl was a famous champion who unhorsed the English champion so easily at a tournament that the English suspected trickery. In the later Middle Ages the Crawfords were one of the greatest families in Scotland: there were about 100 landed families of the name Lindsay, though not all of them acknowledged Crawford as their chief. In general they remained loyal to the Stewarts while indulging in frightful feuds with neighbours such as the Ogilvies, and quarrelling among themselves (the 8th Earl narrowly escaped death at the hands of his son). A younger son of the 10th Earl was the ancestor of the earls of Balcarres (created 1650), who inherited the Crawford title and the chiefship in the 19th century. Lindsay is also a famous name in Scottish literature. Sir David Lindsay (1490–1555), Lyon King of Arms in the reign of James III, was the author of *Ane Satyre of the Three Estaits*, in the Scots vernacular. He was descended from a younger son of a 14th-century Laird of Crawford, a line that also produced the earls of Lindsay (created 1633).

Livingstone

MOTTO
Si je puis
If I can

The name derives from the district in West Lothian, and Lowlanders often spelled it, like the town, without the final 'e'. Sir William Livingstone acquired the barony of Callander and his descendants included the 1st Lord Livingstone in the 15th century. The 5th Lord Livingstone and his son were associated with Mary, Queen of Scots, and James VI made the 7th Lord Livingstone Earl of Linlithgow in 1600. The 4th Earl fought in the Jacobite rising of 1715 and lost the title, as did the earls of Callander, a separate line descended from the 1st Earl of Linlithgow. The origin of the Highland Livingstones is uncertain, and the legend that links them with their Lowland namesakes cannot be trusted. They were called *Mac an Léigh*, 'son of the physician', which tends to confirm an alleged connection with the Beatons. The name was first anglicized as MacLeay, later as Livingstone (the entomology is somewhat perverse). The MacLeays were hereditary keepers of the staff of St. Moluag on the holy isle of Lismore, at the entrance to Loch Linnhe, possibly their original Highland habitat although they were also found in other parts. The great explorer, David Livingstone, born in a miserable tenement in Blantyre, was the grandson of a tenant farmer on the island of Ulva, Argyll.

Logan (MacLennan)

MOTTO
Dum spiro spero
While I breath I hope

The Logans of the Lowlands are traditionally linked with the Highland MacLennans, largely on the basis of colourful but unreliable legend. The origins of the names appear to be different. The MacLennans of Ross were connected with the MacRaes and were standard bearers to the Seaforth Mackenzies in the 17th century. In the south, two knights named Logan accompanied Douglas ('the good Sir James') on his journey to the Holy Land and died with him crusading in Spain in 1329. Somewhat later, the most prominent family was the Logans of Restalrig, outside Edinburgh, who for some time held Fast Castle, west of St. Abb's Head, later held by the Homes. In modern times, James Logan was the author of *The Scottish Gael* (1831), the first work in English to attempt a history of Highland dress.

Logan (MacLennan)

MacAlister

MOTTO
Fortiter
Boldly

The MacAlisters of Loup, a name meaning 'bend' which apparently referred to a feature of their territory, were a branch of Clan

Donald, being descended from a great-grandson of Somerled, ancestor of Clan Donald. They lived in Kintyre, where Charles MacAlister was appointed steward by James III in 1485, and spread into Arran and Bute. Notable cadet branches were MacAlister of Tarbert, hereditary constables of the castle of Tarbert on the border between Kintyre and Knapdale, and MacAlister of Menstrie, who became earls of Stirling, recognized by some MacAlisters as chief of the clan. The MacAlisters of Loup were supporters of the Stewart kings, and fought in James II's army at the Battle of the Boyne (1690). In the 18th century, marriage to a Somervill heiress brought them the estate of Kennox in Strathclyde, henceforth the seat of the chief. The MacAlisters of Tarbert lost their property in 1745.

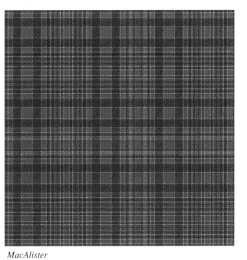
MacAlister

MacArthur

MOTTO
Fide et opera
By fidelity and labour

The MacArthurs came from Argyll and were probably of the same stock as the Campbells. They claimed to be descended from the legendary King Arthur of the Round Table, and if that is hard to swallow, it is no more so than the claim of a Campbell genealogist to have traced his ancestors back to the Egyptian pharaohs. The people who became the Campbells shared with the future MacArthurs the name of *Ua Duibhne*. However, MacArthur was also the name of the hereditary pipers of the MacDonalds. The MacArthurs of Loch Awe

supported Bruce in the war of independence and benefited as a result, at the expense of the MacDougalls of Lorne, who had chosen the wrong side. They also became keepers of Dunstaffnage Castle. The efforts of King James I to subdue the clans hit the MacArthurs hard. Their chief, Iain MacArthur, said to have commanded 1,000 men, was executed (1427) and practically all of his lands confiscated.

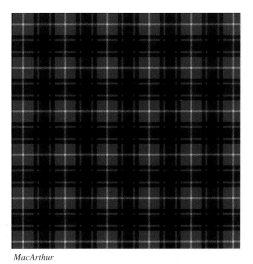
MacArthur

MacAulay

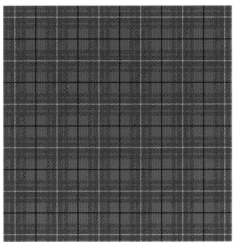

MOTTO
Dulce periculum
Danger is sweet

Amlaidh Mac Amlaidh (Aulay MacAulay) lived in the 13th century and was probably the descendant of a younger son of the Earl of Lennox. He is regarded as the ancestor of the MacAulays of Ardincaple, near southern Loch Lomond, who had links with the Earl of Lennox

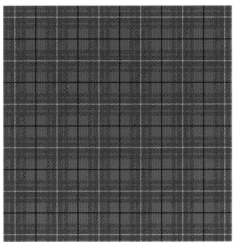
MacAulay

and considered themselves members of *Síol Alpin*. Their badge is a pine tree, and they appear to have been kin to the MacGregors. They were thus potentially threatened by the Campbells, although they kept their land and identity until after the Forty-Five, when the Chief was forced to sell out to the Campbells. They have no connection with the MacAulays of Lewis, whose name meant 'son of Olaf', presumably Olaf the Black, the Norse King of Man and the Western Isles. They were attached to the MacLeods, and possibly originated on the mainland, around Ullapool (Olaf's Palace), although the mainland MacAulays regarded themselves as a sept of the MacAulays of Lewis. Other offshoots of the MacAulays of Lewis were to be found in Sutherland and Ross.

Above
The MacArthurs were keepers of Dunstaffnage Castle, in Strathclyde, which was once the stronghold of both the MacDougalls and the Campbells.

MacBean (MacBain)

MOTTO
Touch not a catt bot
a targe

*A*lthough Clan chiefs can be traced to the 15th century, the origin of the name is unknown though, as a result, there are plenty of theories. Towards the end of the Middle Ages, there were MacBeans in the region of Inverness under the protection of the Mackintosh. According to tradition, they had moved into Clan Chattan territory some time earlier as a result of intermarriage. The MacBeans were great warriors and feature in accounts of many notable battles. Several fell fighting for the Lord of the Isles at Harlaw (1411). Aeneas MacBean of Kinchyle (the leading family) supported the Mackintosh in the Jacobite rising of 1715, and

his brother, Gillies, was killed at Culloden in 1746 after single-handedly despatching 14 Hanoverian dragoons. A descendant, William MacBean, serving in the Sutherland Highlanders, won the Victoria Cross during the Indian Mutiny.

MacBean (MacBain)

MacCallum (Malcolm)

MOTTO
In ardua tendit
He has attempted
difficult things

MacCallum and Malcolm, according to some theories, are two distinct names, but both appear to derive from 'Colm', no less a figure than St. Columba, who brought Christianity to Scotland in the sixth century. An 18th-century MacCallum chief, Alexander MacCallum of Poltalloch (the family that held the chiefship from the late 16th century), changed his name to Malcolm under the asumption that it was simply a different version of the same name, but recent Gaelic scholars have argued that, whereas the MacCallums were the 'sons of Colm', the Malcolms were 'followers' or 'devotees of Colm', since *maol* means 'shaven-headed', i.e. a monk. The MacCallum came from Lorne and were vassals of the Campbells. In the 15th century, Ranald MacCallum received lands in Craignish from Duncan Campbell of Duntrune, who also made him hereditary Constable of Craignish Castle. A notable MacCallum hero was Zachary MacCallum of Poltalloch who, legend says, encountered a party of MacDonalds in 1647, most of whom he killed. He was about to assault their leader, who was none other than the redoubtable Alasdair MacColla, Montrose's guerilla leader, when he was treacherously cut down from behind. John Malcolm of Poltalloch became Lord Malcolm in 1896, but the title expired with him in 1902.

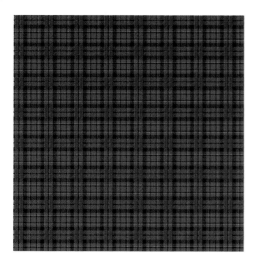

MacCallum

MacDonald

MOTTO
Per mare per terras
By sea and by land

MacDonald

Can Donald, the greatest of the Highland clans, was originally one, but some branches became substantial, independent clans themselves. The name MacDonell is simply a variant. The original Donald was the grandson of Somerled, who built up his principality in Argyll, including Arran and Bute and the southerly Inner Hebrides, at the expense of the Norse King of the Isles, partly by force and partly by his marriage to a daughter of King Olaf of Man. Though a vassal of both the Lord of the Isles and the King of Scots, he was in fact an independent ruler of comparable power, although his challenge to the King of Scots ended in his defeat and death (1164). His lands were divided among his sons: Dugall, ancestor of Clan Dougall, gained the Argyll mainland and adjacent isles; Ranald received Kintyre and Islay; Angus, Bute, which passed to the Stewarts through marriage two generations later. Ranald's possessions were divided between his own two sons, with Donald receiving the southern isles including Islay, the core of the future Lordship of the Isles. After the wars of independence, the MacDonalds (not, of course, yet so called) benefited at the expense of the MacDougalls of Mull, who had supported John Balliol against Bruce, and also from the destruction of the Comyns. Angus Óg, Donald's grandson, commanded the isles

from Islay to Ardnamurchan, plus part of Lochaber.

He may be regarded as the first **MacDonald of the Isles**, his son John, or Iain, becoming 1st Lord of the Isles. He gained Lewis by royal grant and the southern half of the Outer Hebrides by inheritance through his wife, plus Rhum, and Moidart and Knoydart on the mainland. As a dynast, John of Islay could have taught even the Bourbons a thing or two. Having got rid of his productive first wife, he married a daughter of the future King Robert II, which eventually brought him Kintyre and Knapdale. His territories were now considerably larger than the old Norse Kingdom of the Isles and in 1354 he conferred on himself the title *Dominus Insularum* (Lord of the Isles). Donald, 2nd Lord of the Isles, married a daughter of the Earl of Ross, whose holdings were second only to his own. On the Earl's death, his legal successor was his daughter, but the Regent, the Duke of Albany, secured it for her uncle, the Earl of Buchan, who was also his son. This provoked the famous campaign which ended in the Battle of Harlaw (1411). The Lord of the Isles was a threat to the King of Scots, and James's efforts to crush the Highlanders provoked a series of rebellions in the west, though he eventually accepted the inheritance of the Ross earldom by Alexander, 3rd Lord of the Isles, on the death of his mother. The long contest with the Crown could, in retrospect, have only one ending. The 4th Lord, John, was involved in a conspiracy with the English (frequent but unsatisfactory allies) and the Earl of Douglas against the Crown and as a result lost the earldom of Ross and other territories, including Kintyre. His illegitimate son, another Angus Óg, refused to accept this, but was weakened by a split in loyalty, with the MacDonalds mostly following Angus Óg and others, including the MacLeans and Mackintoshes, remaining loyal to the 4th Lord. Angus Óg also found himself in opposition to the (Campbell) Earl of Argyll, his father-in-law. He was murdered in 1490, but another leader of the Islesmen appeared in Alexander of Lochalsh, his first cousin, who captured Inverness before being defeated by the Mackenzies. In 1493 the lordship was officially annexed to the Crown, though that did not end the conflict and Donald Dubh, son of Angus Óg, spent half a century in ultimately futile revolt. By his death in 1546, the western clans, once held together by the Lords of the Isles, had become independent and often mutually hostile units.

MacDonald of Sleat

The first **MacDonald of Sleat** was Hugh, youngest son of Alexander, 3rd Lord of the Isles. He received Sleat, on Skye, from his father. As in other Highland dynasties, the persistence of the family name, Donald, can be a source of confusion. Donald Gorm, 5th of Sleat, was involved in efforts to regain the inheritance of the lordship in 1539, and was killed besieging the Mackenzie castle of Eilean Donan. After the death of Donald Dubh, MacDonald of Sleat was the senior line, and Donald Gorm Mór, 7th of Sleat, described himself in a letter to Elizabeth I of England as 'Lord of the Isles of Scotland and Chief of the whole Clan of Donald Irishmen wheresoever'. However, he was reconciled to the King of Scots, and henceforth the MacDonalds remained, with some exceptions, loyal

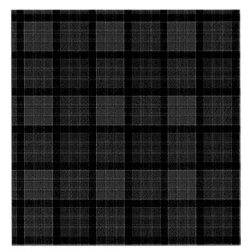

MacDonald of Clan Ranald

supporters of the Stewart dynasty. The only serious exception occurred in 1745, when the current chief, Alexander, declined to raise his men in support of Prince Charles Edward. His successor, also Alexander, was created Lord MacDonald in 1796. A son of the 1st Lord inherited an estate at Bosville in Yorkshire, and his younger brother became the 2nd Lord MacDonald. This led to a curious division of honours in the present century, when the representative of the Yorkshire branch (who had

adopted the name Bosville) regained the chiefship of MacDonald of Sleat, while the current Lord MacDonald remained chief of the Name (i.e. of Clan Donald).

The founder of **MacDonald of Clan Ranald** was Ranald, eldest son of the 1st Lord of the Isles by his first wife. (Ranald did not inherit the lordship, which

chiefship. It was provoked by an attempt on the part of the Frasers to secure the Clan Ranald chiefship for a candidate of their choosing. As the opposing forces prepared for battle, the Earl of Argyll stepped in to prevent it, but on their way home the Frasers were ambushed by Clan Ranald north of Loch Lochy, and frightful slaughter ensued. As it was a hot day, both sides threw their plaids aside (probably a common practice whatever the weather), hence the name, the Battle of the Shirts. In spite of this and other losses, Clan Ranald remained in possession of their lands and played a prominent part in the national conflicts of the 17th–18th centuries. The lands were confiscated after Culloden, but later restored, and in the end it was not violence but criminal negligence that brought ruin. In 1794 the 17th Chief was succeeded by his worthless grandson, who squandered his immense resources so thoroughly in the gaming saloons of London that the lands were sold to sheep-rearing landlords.

The ruined but still oppressive castle of Invergarry, overlooking Loch Oich, was the stronghold of **MacDonell of Glengarry**. This was a cadet branch of MacDonald of Clan Ranald, stemming from Donald, son of Ranald. In spite of the cantankerous nature of many Glengarry chiefs, they generally shared Clan Ranald's loyalties. The 6th Glengarry married a daughter of MacDonald of Lochalsh, which gave him a doubtful claim to the chiefship of Clan Donald and involved the clan in a long feud with the expanding Mackenzies. The 9th Glengarry fought with Montrose and was rewarded after the Restoration (1660) with

went to his younger half-brother, whose mother was a daughter of the first Stewart monarch.) For centuries, the stronghold of Clan Ranald was the fortress of Eilean Tioram in Loch Moidart. They were loyal subjects of the Lord of the Isles, but some of the most ferocious violence in which they were involved resulted from fratricidal conflicts. Dugald, 6th Clanranald, was killed by his own kin, and one of the bloodiest battles in Highland history resulted (1544) from a dispute over the

Above

Beautiful and remote Blaven on the Isle of Skye. Hugh, youngest son of Alexander, 3rd Lord of the Isles, received lands on Skye from his father, becoming 1st MacDonald of Sleat.

MacDonell of Glengarry

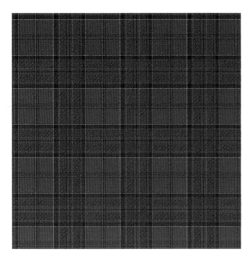

MacDonell of Keppoch

the Restoration (1660) with the title Lord MacDonell and Aros, though the title was subsequently separated from the chiefship. The clan rallied to Prince Charles Edward in 1745, but their leader, son of the Chief, was accidentally killed when a musket went off while being cleaned, and some dispirited Glengarry men subsequently deserted – an indication of the intense loyalty that clans felt towards their leaders. In the desolation that followed Culloden, companies of militia were raised from the impoverished clansmen, and in the 1790s some of these Glengarry Highlanders received assistance to emigrate to Canada. They founded Glengarry in Ontario, and named their homesteads after their old farms. In the War of 1812 they were summoned by the fiery cross to repel a raid by U.S. forces. They perhaps did more than anyone to encourage the strong feelings of clanship in Canada. Meanwhile, the 15th Chief, Colonel Alasdair McDonell of Glengarry, strutted about at home with a large 'tail' of attendants as if he were living in a previous century. His successor, depressed by debt and evictions, sold up and emigrated to Australia.

The **MacDonells of Keppoch** descended from Alastair, third son of John, 1st Lord of the Isles, whose lands were in Lochaber. They took part in the various campaigns and rebellions of the Lords of the Isles, losing some land to the Mackenzies, which added fuel to feud. They remained closely connected with Clan Ranald and Glengarry, in spite of an incident in 1663 when Glengarry failed to avenge the murder of the 12th MacDonell of Keppoch near Invergarry (vengeance was later exacted by MacDonald of Sleat). John, 4th Chief, or Captain, as many

MacDonald chiefs were called, was deposed after handing over one of his men, no doubt for good reason, to the Mackintosh. His successor was a cousin, the builder of Keppoch castle. A successor, the 10th Chief, was the father of the founder of the Canadian line of MacDonells, the Seigneurs de Rigaud, in Quebec. MacDonell of Keppoch was involved in the last serious clan battle in the Highlands, in 1688, against the old enemy, the Mackintosh. It resulted from the Mackintosh having obtained a charter for the lands of Glenroy. Defeated in the battle, he surrendered his claim, but the MacDonells were later invaded by government troops with Mackintosh support. For 40 years the 15th Chief, known as Coll of the Cows, held on to his lands by power of the sword. He and his successors took vigorous part in the Jacobite risings, and Keppoch, one of the few Highland chiefs with military experience, led the first action of the Forty-Five when he intercepted Government forces at Highbridge. He died at Culloden and the estates were forfeit.

The **MacDonalds of Glencoe** were a small clan who derived their lands from Iain Abrach, a brother of the 1st Lord of the Isles, and their chiefs were known as MacIain. They were a small clan, renowned cattle thieves, who preserved their independence in the natural stronghold of Glencoe in spite of the hostility of their powerful neighbour, Campbell of Glenorchy (later Earl of Breadalbane). Through mishaps, MacIain MacDonald was six days past the deadline when, in 1692, he took the oath of submission to the government of William and Mary required to secure a free pardon for earlier resistance. No objections were raised at the time, and no suspicions were aroused in Glencoe when a company of troops was billeted

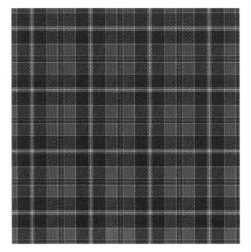

MacDonald of Kingsburgh

on them a few weeks later. They remained two weeks, on friendly terms with their hosts, then turned on them in the night, shooting MacIain in his bed and killing 38 men, women and children. The rest, perhaps 150, escaped up the glen, though some probably died in the snow. The massacre was instigated by the Secretary of State, the Master of Stair, and the order was signed by King William, though he probably did not understand the implications. The troops were commanded by Campbell of Glenlyon, who was in fact related to MacIain MacDonald by marriage, but few of the soldiers were named Campbell; some of them attempted to

Breadalbane apparently had no foreknowledge of the deed. However, the massacre of Glencoe aggravated hostility towards the Campbells and furthered the alienation of the Highlands.

The name **MacDonald of Kingsburgh** is remembered as a result of the romantic episode of 1746, when Prince Charles Edward, on the run from government troops, reached Skye disguised as Flora MacDonald's Irish maid, and subsequently made his escape to France. He spent the night at the house of Alexander MacDonald of Kingsburgh, factor to MacDonald of Sleat, which was occupied by government soldiers. Flora MacDonald, whose stepfather was a tacksman (a tenant, usually also a blood relation) of Sir Alexander MacDonald of Sleat, later married Alexander of Kingsburgh's son, Allen, and they emigrated to North America, where Allen fought against the rebellious colonists in the War of American Independence. They eventually returned to the Hebrides, though by then Kingsburgh had passed into other hands. By no stretch of the imagination was there a Clan MacDonald of Kingsburgh, but there is a tartan. According to hallowed tradition, the sett derives from a tartan waistcoat which was given to Prince Charles Edward by his host on Skye in 1746.

MacDougall

MOTTO
Buaidh no bas
To conquer or die

The MacDougalls, once a formidable power in the west, still hold part of their ancient patrimony in Lorne. They are senior to Clan Donald, being descended from Dugall, eldest son of Somerled. He was the senior sub-king under the Norse King of the Isles and styled himself 'of Argyll'. Necessarily, the future MacDougalls were a sea power, and their original strongholds were Dunstaffnage, which later passed to the Campbells, and Dunollie, above Oban Bay, which they still hold. In 1263, when Haakon of Norway set out to re-establish Norwegian sovereignty in the Western Isles, Dugall's grandson elected to support the King

of Scots, which turned out to be the right decision as Haakon was defeated at Largs. During the wars of independence, however, the MacDougalls, connected by marriage with the Comyns, were on the wrong side; in fact they were at one time a greater threat to Bruce than were the English. With Bruce victorious, the MacDougall estates were bestowed on the MacDonalds and others. The great days were over, but the 6th Chief regained the lordship of Lorne and, although that title passed to the Stewarts on his death, the MacDougall chiefship fell to a cousin whose family had supported Bruce and held the castle of Dunollie. The MacDougalls did not lose hope of regaining all their lands, but they were up against the power of the Campbells. The fall of the Earl of Argyll in 1686 appeared to offer an opportunity, but the moment passed, and Dunollie itself was forfeit, though later returned, as a result of MacDougall engagement in the Jacobite cause.

MacDougall

Below
The palace of Scone, Perthshire. The descendants of the MacDuff enjoyed many privileges, among them the right to enthrone the King of Scots at Scone.

MacDuff

MOTTO
Deus juvat
God assists

The origins of the ancient and exalted Clan MacDuff can be traced back to the earls of Fife in the early 12th century and, by inference, a great deal further. The first documented Earl of Fife was the eldest son of Malcolm Ceann Mór (the MacDuff of Shakespeare's *Macbeth* cannot be historically established although he is certainly feasible). He was also hereditary abbot of Dunkeld and his wife was a granddaughter of Queen Gruoch (Lady Macbeth) and sister of the ruler of Moray. His descendants enjoyed unique privileges, among them the right to enthrone the King of Scots at Scone. Fife remained the centre of MacDuff power, although they also owned land farther north and in Lothian. The line of the old Celtic earls ended in the 14th century, and the modern earls and dukes of Fife appear to be unrelated to them, at least directly. The representatives of the ancient line were acknowledged in the 18th century to be the earls of Wemyss, whose descent from Gillemichael MacDuff, one of the first documented earls of Fife in the early 12th century, if not proven, is highly probable.

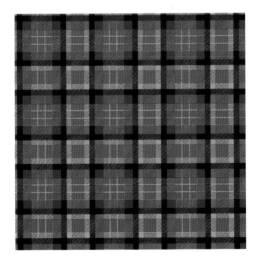

MacDuff

MacEwen

MOTTO
Reviresco
I grow strong
again

MacEwen

The MacEwens seem once to have been a numerous clan, connected with the MacNeils and MacLachlans. In the 18th-century parish records of Kilfinnan in Argyll there is a mention of a ruined building on Loch Fyne which was named MacEwen's Castle, for a chief who held land in the district of Otter. There appears to have been no other memory of the MacEwens in their own homeland even at that time. The name and its many variants, such as Ewing and, possibly, McOwan, is fairly common today, but firm connections with the MacEwens of Otter are hard to establish. The first known chief lived in the early 13th century, and many of his successors are recorded down to the 9th and last chief, Swene, in the early 15th century. The demise of the clan resulted from the lands passing to the Campbells of Argyll as a result of legal arrangements in which the Campbells were so much more adept than their less sophisticated neighbours. The hereditary bards of the leading Campbell families were MacEwens, and others are mentioned as vassals of the earls of Argyll. A party of MacEwens were said to have come from Skye to participate in the Jacobite rising of 1715, but their connection with the MacEwens of Otter is unknown.

MacFarlane

MOTTO
This I'll defend

The MacFarlanes were descended from the old Celtic earls of Lennox and through them, probably, from the kings of Munster. Their homeland was Arrochar, at the head of Loch Long, and their name derived from the 4th Chief, Párlan (Bartholomew), descendant of Gilchrist, who received the lands from his brother, Earl Malduin. They were confirmed by royal charter in 1420. When the last earl of Lennox was executed by James I, MacFarlane had a claim to the earldom. Instead it went to the Stewarts of Darnley, but trouble was averted by a MacFarlane-Stewart marriage and thereafter the MacFarlanes remained loyal to the Stewarts. They were warlike raiders, at odds with their neighbours around Loch Lomond, and were often active by the light of 'MacFarlane's lantern' (i.e. the Moon). Their pipe tune is called 'Lifting the Cattle'. Although early converts to Protestantism, the MacFarlanes opposed the Covenanters and fought with Montrose in the civil wars. When their castle of Inveruglas, on an island in Loch Lomond, was destroyed by Cromwell's forces, the chief moved to a house in Arrochar. The 20th Chief, Walter (died 1767), a friend of James Boswell, was one of the few who endeavoured to preserve the Gaelic heritage by collecting and transcribing documents. He was once addressed by the English General Wade (the Government's

MacFarlane

commander in Scotland after the Fifteen) as 'Mr MacFarlane', which in England would have been more courteous than plain 'MacFarlane'. Indignantly he explained, ' "Mr MacFarlane" may with equal propriety be said to many; but I, and only I, am MacFarlane.' Not long afterwards a black swan was observed among MacFarlane's white swans. An ancient prophecy predicted that such an event presaged the loss of Arrochar, and the 21st Chief was forced to sell up a few years later.

MacGillivray

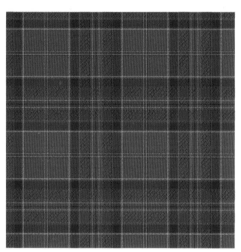

MOTTO
Touch not
this cat

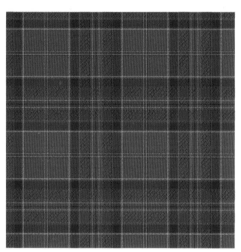

MacGillivray

The Clan is said to have originated in Mull, and some became followers of MacLean of Duart. Another group sought protection from the Mackintosh chief in the mid-13th century, an early example of a process that resulted in the development of the Clan Chattan confederation. The presumed progenitor was Gillebride, or Gillivray, and by the 15th century his descendants held land in Dunmaglas in Strathnairn. The Clan expanded, producing many cadet branches and eventually forming one of the main constituents of Clan Chattan. At Culloden, Clan Chattan was led by Alexander MacGillivray of Dunmaglas. They threw back Cumberland's left wing before, hurling stones at the enemy, they were forced to retreat. Casualties were frightful. A stone still marks the Well of the Dead where the MacGillivray chief,

mortally wounded, died as he drank. Poverty compelled his successor to enlist in the army. His son, who was chief for nearly 70 years, bequeathed the land to his tenants, but that did not prevent it being broken up and sold a few years later.

MacGregor

MOTTO
'S rioghal mo dhream
My race is royal

The MacGregors were the principal members of *Síol Alpin*, the kin of Kenneth MacAlpin, claiming descent from his brother or son. Their homeland was Glenorchy, where, through marriage, the Campbells had a foothold by the 14th century. By one means or another, they steadily extended their possessions and the MacGregor chiefs became their tenants. Besides depriving them of legal title to the land, the Campbells attempted to establish their own nominee as overall chief of Clan MacGregor. The MacGregors, the 'Children of the Mist', were gradually forced into a lawless existence, defending their land by the sword and alienating their neighbours. Several commissions of fire and sword against them were granted by the Government and, following their massacre of the Colquhouns at Glenfruin, the MacGregors were proscribed by edict of the privy council under James VI (1603). The chief and a number of leading men were executed and the very name was banned. The MacGregors adopted a variety of *nommes de guerre*, including Campbell, a source of future problems for genealogists and, no doubt, unwittingly misplaced loyalties among later generations. The ferocity of the government against the MacGregors had no limit. On occasion, they were hunted with bloodhounds, and a new commission issued to the Earl of Argyll against them in 1611 authorized the branding of women in the face with a red-hot key. The laws against the MacGregors lasted, with remissions, until 1774, although they were enforced only sporadically and many clans were sympathetic, notably the Grants and Mackenzies, who were usually prepared to shelter them, if necessary, at some risk to

themselves. As MacGregors fought under Montrose, and later against Cromwell, the proscription was lifted at the Restoration (1660), but it was reimposed after the rebellion against William III in 1689.

The oldest MacGregor tartan is known as Rob Roy, after the most famous of the MacGregor outlaws. A son of the 15th Chief and his Campbell wife, he was born in 1671, when the proscription of the Clan had been temporarily lifted. Although his romantic image derives from Scott's novel and the effusiveness of moviemakers, he was certainly involved in many adventurous episodes and was no mere bandit but a man of education and culture. He died in his bed, at peace with the world, in 1734.

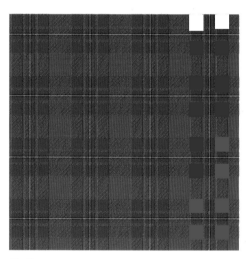

MacGregor

Opposite
A statue of Rob Roy MacGregor in Stirling. Born in 1671 he was the most famous of the MacGregor outlaws. His romantic image derives mainly from Sir Walter Scott's novel. However, he did partake in many adventures and was rather more than a mere bandit. He was well educated and a man of culture who died peacefully in his bed in 1734.

Left
The SS Sir Walter Scott on Lake Katrine in the Trossachs is named after the famous Scottish romantic writer. Scott immortalized Rob Roy MacGregor in his famous novel.

MacIntyre

MOTTO
Per ardua
Through difficulties

MacIntyre

MacInnes

MOTTO
Ghift dhe Agus an righ
By the grace of God and king

Can MacInnes was of ancient origin, and they were probably connected with the MacGillivrays; a 17th-century chronicler described them as the same people. Their paths subsequently diverged, the sons of Innes, or Angus, coming under Campbell, rather than Mackintosh, protection. The ruins of their castle of Kinlochaline still stand, and a MacInnes was still its constable when it was besieged by Alasdair MacColla (MacDonald) in 1645. The name also occurred elsewhere. The hereditary bowmen to the Mackinnon chief were named MacInnes, but the origin of their name appears to be different. Unlike the MacInneses of Kinlochaline, they were Jacobites, as were a third group who were followers of Stewart of Ardshiel and fought among the 'men of Appin' at Culloden. They are thought to have been a 15th-century branch of MacInnes of Kinlochaline.

Colourful legends account for the origin of Clan MacIntyre and for its name. The Gaelic name, *Mac-an t'saor* means 'son of the carpenter', which might well have been applied to people not related by blood. They were closely connected with the MacDonalds and one legend says that their founder was a MacDonald who cut off his thumb to plug a leak in his boat so that he could wave both arms for help. Wood certainly seems to have been a significant material: the hereditary foresters to the Stewart and later Campbell lords of Lorne were MacIntyres (they included the famous bard, Donald Bán MacIntyre, 1724–1812), but so were the Mackenzie pipers. Their homeland was Glenoe, north of Ben Cruachan, a MacIntyre mountain (and war cry) as well as the Campbells'. However, the Campbells were their landlords, and the substitution of cash for the previous symbolic rent of a snowball presaged their decline. The last of their land was lost in 1806, and many emigrated to the United States. Besides the Clan Chattan group, there were others elsewhere, possibly unrelated.

MacInnes

Mackay

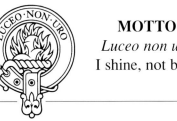

MOTTO
Manu forti
With a strong
hand

The Mackays claimed descent from the old earls or *mormaers* (a weightier title than the English 'earl') of Moray, although their homeland was in the north, centred on Strathnaver. Their movement thither was possibly the result of the campaigns of King Malcolm IV (1153-1165). It was said that in 1427 their Chief, Angus Dubh, who was married to a daughter of Donald, 2nd Lord of the Isles, could command 4,000 men. That might be an exaggeration, but in 1626 his successor, who was later created Lord Reay, took 3,000 men to fight for the Protestants in the Thirty Years' War. The Mackays were famous warriors, and the chieftain of a cadet branch commanded the army defeated at Killiecrankie in 1689. Although they were on the periphery of Highland conflict, the Mackays were always under pressure from the earls of Sutherland, a title that passed to the powerful Gordons in the early 16th century, and they eventually became vassals of the Earl of Huntly and took part in his assault on the Sinclair earls of Caithness. As Whigs and Protestants, they survived the disturbances of the 18th century, but succumbed to the destructive processes that followed the defeat of Jacobitism. The earls, later dukes, of Sutherland were inveterate 'improvers', and the Sutherland Clearances are infamous. Their mark remains on the under-

Mackay

populated north to this day. What remained of the Mackay inheritance was sold by the 7th Lord Reay in 1829. The old chiefly line ended in 1875, and the chiefship was inherited by the Mackays of the Netherlands, a distinguished family (one of whom became Dutch prime minister) who had settled there in the 17th century.

Mackenzie

MOTTO
Luceo non uro
I shine, not burn

Mackenzie

Since the 'k' in Mackenzie is an intruder, not present in Gaelic, Mackenzie is one of those names generally spelled without a capital letter following the Mac. The origins of the Clan are unknown, though a strong tradition links them with the old royal house of Lorne. They were a major constituent of Clan Chattan. A royal charter of 1362, which confirms the current Chief, Murdoch, in the lands of Kintail, corroborates his descent from Gilleon of the Aird, a prince of the house of Lorne. Murdoch's descendant, Alasdair of Kintail, benefited by his support of the Crown against the MacDonald Lord of the Isles. Alasdair's grandson, Iain, led the Mackenzies at Flodden (1513), and was one of the few chiefs to escape the slaughter. In general, Mackenzie chiefs were remarkably durable: Iain also survived the action at Pinkie, 35 years later. The Mackenzies continued to be strong supporters of the Stewart dynasty, and were

probably involved in the Battle of Langside for Mary, Queen of Scots, though her defeat brought them no harm, perhaps because they were quick to make their submission to the Regent, the Earl of Moray. The Mackenzies were now a powerful force in the Highlands, benefiting from the decline of Clan Donald and often managing to avoid the damaging feuds that weakened other clans. They prised Lewis from the MacLeods, Lochalsh from the MacDonells of Glengarry, and by the 17th century controlled territory stretching from the Outer Hebrides to the Black Isle. In 1623 the Mackenzie became earls of Seaforth, but that loyalty to the Stewart dynasty which had been a major factor in their rise was also their ruin. The 4th Earl died in exile with James VII and II. The 5th Earl was attainted after the rising of 1715, losing lands and title. He regained some of his lands, though not the title, in 1726. Mackenzies also fought in the Forty-Five though not as a clan. The Seaforth earldom was recreated in 1771 and the lost estates regained by purchase, but the decline, closely following the prophecies of a 16th-century Mackenzie wise man, known as the Brahan Seer, continued. Problematic succession resulted in the loss of the title and, eventually, most of the land through marriages to steadily less substantial heiresses, although the Mackenzie earls of Cromarty held on to one portion. The original estate of Kintail is today held by the National Trust for Scotland.

Mackinnon

MOTTO
Audentes fortuna juvat
Fortune assists the daring

The Mackinnons claim descent both from the family of Kenneth MacAlpin and from St. Columba, and significantly the brother of a 14th-century chief was the Abbot of Iona. The last abbot, who died in 1500 (his effigy can still be seen on Iona), was Iain Mackinnon. The Mackinnon homeland was the Isle of Mull, but they acquired, presumably through marriage, a larger area at Strathaird on Skye, plus Scalpay. Their castle of Dunakin (Dunan) guarded the passage between the two islands. The chiefs were important officials under the Lord of the Isles, and they took part in the efforts to restore the lordship after its suppression in 1493, but by the 17th century were loyal subjects of the Stewarts. The lands were forfeit after the Fifteen, restored, lost again after the Forty-Five, and the last of them sold to pay off debts. The last chief of the direct line died in poverty in 1808.

Mackinnon

Mackintosh

MOTTO
Touch not the cat
bot a glove

In Gaelic, the name means 'son of the chief', and it was therefore no doubt applied to others besides members of the famous clan which led the confederation known as Clan Chattan. It first appears as the name of a captain of Clan Chattan in the 15th century, when the chief was based on an island in Loch Moy. He claimed descent from a younger son of MacDuff, ancestor of the old earls of Fife. In spite of the power of the Comyns, the clan supported Bruce during the wars of independence, and fought with the forces of the Regent under the Earl of Mar at Harlaw (1411). The number and intensity of Mackintosh feuds was popularly ascribed to their bad temper, but no doubt had more to do with the responsibilities imposed by leadership of Clan Chattan and by the endless complications over land ownership. Some experts believe that the famous Battle of the Clans at Perth in 1396 was fought between Mackintosh and Comyn. The

Comyns were then no longer as potent a force, and a more formidable opponent was the Gordon Earl of Huntly, who was overlord of some Mackintosh lands in Badenoch. One Mackintosh chief was judicially murdered by Huntly, though his followers had their revenge when they killed the Gordon Earl in battle (1562). Another famous clan battle, often described as the last, took place at Mulroy in 1688, when the Mackintoshes were defeated by MacDonell of Keppoch. Although they did not come out for James VII and II in 1689, they were active in the rising of 1715, when a famous leader, Mackintosh of Borlum, led a Jacobite force as far as Preston in Lancashire. The Mackintosh himself lost his estates but regained them before his death in 1731. For the next hundred years, the succession never once passed from father to son and ultimately went abroad (though it has since returned). Angus, 23rd Chief, was an officer in the British army in 1745, but his wife, 'Colonel Anne', raised the clan for Prince Charles Edward. She engineered the exploit known as the Rout of Moy, when a large Government force was defeated by a handful of Mackintosh retainers.

Mackintosh

MacLachlan

MOTTO
Fortis et fidus
Brave and faithful

Lachlan, from whom the clan take their name, was according to the Celtic genealogists five generations removed from

MacLachlan

Aodh O'Neill, King of Ulster in the 11th century. His seat was Castle Lachlan on Loch Fyne, and the MacLachlans were close neighbours of the Campbells. Their survival depended on good relations with that powerful clan, and there were frequent marriages between them. One branch were physicians to the Campbell chiefs, another held the Campbell castle of Inchconnel on Loch Awe in the 17th century, and the MacLachlans often acted with the Campbells against other neighbours, notably the Lamonts. Yet, surprisingly, the MacLachlans managed to preserve considerable independence of action, and in the 18th century they were keen Jacobites. Their fighting men were practically wiped out at Culloden, where the elderly chief was shot out of his saddle by a cannon-ball. It is said that his people learned of the disaster when his riderless horse arrived in Strathlachlan, a story that, because of the distance involved, must be consigned to the realm of myth. In spite of their record, the MacLachlans regained their confiscated lands quite quickly through the good offices of the Duke of Argyll, and the castle, bombarded into ruins by a warship in Loch Fyne, was later rebuilt in Scots-Baronial style.

MacLaren

MOTTO
Creag an Tuirc
The boar's rock

The MacLarens are not well documented, but it is generally accepted that they came from Balquhidder and were related to the old

Right

Iona Abbey. A branch of the chiefly family of Mackinnon were hereditary abbots of Iona, the last of which was the 9th Chief Iain Mackinnon who was also Bishop of the Isles. He died around 1500.

Page 79

The ownership of Duart lands has a turbulent history with the Campbells eventually taking over all MacLean territory. However, Sir Fitzroy MacLean regained Duart in 1911 and restored the imposing fortress on the Sound of Mull.

earls of Strathearn, the last of whom died in the mid-14th century. They spread a considerable distance, though they never held legal title to their lands, but in the 16th century they were overrun by the MacGregors with terrible slaughter and, probably, the destruction of all clan records. The clan never really recovered, but survived under the protection of Campbell of Glenorchy. They were also connected with the Stewarts of Appin, whose founder, according to legend, was a son of the Stewart Lord of Lorne by the famously beautiful daughter of a MacLaren chieftain. The military tradition of the MacLarens is slightly better documented. They were notable mercenaries, fighting for the French in the 15th century and with the Swedes in the Thirty Years' War. They were loyal to the Stewarts during the civil wars of the 17th century and took part in the major Jacobite risings. The adventures of a MacLaren officer captured after Culloden provided Sir Walter Scott with stirring material for *Redgauntlet*. The chiefship had died out but was later re-established and the old clan gathering place of *Creag an Tuirc* (the Rock of the Boar) in Balquhidder, was regained by purchase.

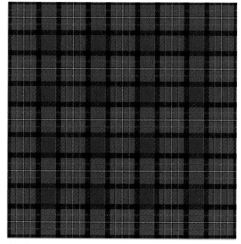

MacLaren

MacLean

MOTTO
Virtue mine
honour

The ancestor from whom the MacLeans took their name was Gillean of the Battle-Axe, a 13th-century chieftain probably

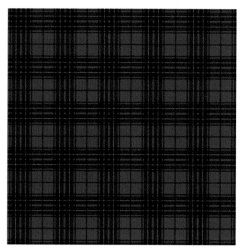

MacLean Hunting

descended from the royal house of Lorne. There were two senior branches, MacLean of Duart and MacLaine of Lochbuie, founded by two brothers who lived in the late 14th century. In addition, other cadet branches became virtually independent, and occasionally hostile, clans, notably the MacLeans of Ardgour, founded by a son of Red Hector of the Battles, the famous warrior who fell at Harlaw (1411), and the MacLeans of Coll, whose ancestor was another son of Red Hector. The MacLeans of Ardgour, in Morvern, still live in Ardgour House, but the last MacLean of Coll sold up and emigrated to South Africa in the 19th century.

Among MacLean tartans today, the most interesting is the MacLean Hunting Tartan. In 1587 a charter of land on Islay, then held by a son of MacLean of Duart, mentions the feudal duty, payable in cloth of white, black and green. The same colours were mentioned 100 years later. They are the colours of the Hunting Tartan.

MacLean of Duart

MacLean of Duart is generally regarded as the senior house, though there was always some rivalry. In important affairs, the

MacLeans normally acted together, but the house of Duart generally stood higher with the Lords of the Isles, in whose service they held many military and civil posts. In the civil war caused by the revolt of Angus Óg against his father, the 4th Lord, the MacLeans remained loyal to the father, at heavy cost, in the Battle of Bloody Bay (1480), when 50 MacLeans who had sought shelter in a cave were smoked out and slaughtered. After the death of Donald Dubh, the Macleans became good subjects of the Stewart dynasty while pursuing their feud with Clan Donald, the chief beneficiaries of which were the Campbells. The Campbells eventually took over all the Duart territory by various means, including English warships. Sir Fitzroy Maclean, who as a young man took part in the charge of the Light Brigade, regained Duart after a lifetime of endeavour in 1911 and restored the great fortress on the Sound of Mull. His namesake, the late Sir Fitzroy MacLean of Strachur, belonged to the house of Ardgour.

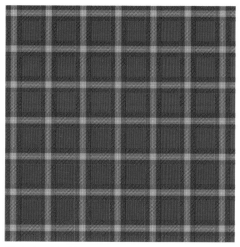

MacLaine of Lochbuie

The impending death of a **MacLaine of Lochbuie** is said to be signalled by the appearance of a headless horseman, the ghost of Ewen, son of Chief Iain Óg, who was the subject of a sombre gothic tale of the rivalry of Lochbuie and Duart. In spite of internecine rivalry, both branches were vassals of the Lord of the Isles and fought for the Stewarts in the civil wars of the 17th century, though Lochbuie did not take part in the Jacobite rising of 1745. The MacLaines held Lochbuie for some time after Duart was lost, and the fortune amassed in the tea trade by the 20th Chief in the 19th century staved off the debtors for a few generations, though the land was eventually lost in the 20th century.

MacLeod

MOTTO
Hold fast

Leod was a son of Olaf the Black (died 1237), the Norse king of Man and the Isles. He acquired Harris, Lewis and part of Skye, including Dunvegan, the home of the chiefs for 700 years. His sons, Tormod and Torquil, were the ancestors of the two senior branches of the MacLeods, *Síol Thormoid*, on Harris, and *Síol Thorcail*, on Lewis. As with the MacLeans, there was rivalry between the two over seniority (in Celtic custom, the eldest son did not have automatic precedence), but after the disasters that overcame the MacLeods of Lewis in the 16th century, MacLeod of Harris and of Dunvegan, was unchallenged. Thanks to

MacLeod

the impregnability of Dunvegan, which could only be entered from the sea, the MacLeod archives are unrivalled among Highland clans and their history is well known.

An early title of **MacLeod of Harris** was 'of Glenelg', across the bay from Skye, for which, unlike most MacLeod lands, they held a royal charter (1343). From the 15th century they were styled 'of Dunvegan'. They were vassals of both the Lord of the Isles and the King of Scots, but fought with the former on the expedition that culminated in the Battle of Harlaw (1411). The 8th Chief, Alasdair Crotach (died 1547) engaged in fierce battles with Clan Ranald, and twice resorted to the MacLeods'

secret weapon, the Fairy Flag, which must only be unfurled in a desperate situation (still at Dunvegan, it has been identified as a Byzantine banner, brought from Constantinople in the 11th century). After the collapse of the lordship of the Isles, Dunvegan became the centre of Gaelic culture. There would be found, besides the leaders of many septs of *Síol Thormoid*, bards, harpers, jesters, members of the learned Beatons and visitors from England and the Continent. Chiefs such as Rory Mór, who was knighted by James VI, built schools and roads, instituted an Edinburgh post, and imported grain for their tenants when the harvest was bad. The MacLeods lost about 500 men at the Battle of Worcester in 1651 fighting for Charles II, a sacrifice that produced an ironic benefit because the MacLeods never took the field for the royal Stewarts again. Thus they escaped the destruction of the Forty-Five, and when Samuel Johnson and James Boswell visited Dunvegan in 1773 they were royally entertained and delighted to see 'a great Highland laird surrounded by so many of his clan'. The MacLeods could not avoid the fate that overtook the Highland clans in the 19th century, but the spirit of the clan was revived in a remarkable way by Dame Flora MacLeod, who became chief in 1935. Under her benign hospitality, the annual clan gathering became an international affair, attracting descendants of the scattered clansfolk from all over the world.

By the 14th century **MacLeod of Lewis** was in possession of Assynt in Sutherland, as well as Lewis, the origin of one of many powerful and quarrelsome septs. Another held the island of Raasay in the 16th century when the MacLeods of Lewis fell victim to the Mackenzies. Like their kin in

Harris, they held no legal title to their lands, which gave James VI the excuse to grant Lewis to a commercial company, the Fife Adventurers, as though the MacLeods did not exist. The Adventurers were sent packing by the MacLeods, but sold their rights to Mackenzie of Kintail, who had long harboured designs on Lewis and had acquired MacLeod possessions on the mainland. The Mackenzies proved more formidable than the Fife Adventurers, and virtually destroyed the clan, the whole chiefly family being executed. Only Raasay survived, and when Samuel Johnson and James Boswell visited the island in 1773, they found the chief 'a perfect representation of a Highland gentleman'. However, debts were piling up, the clansmen were emigrating, and in 1846 the chief sold up and followed them.

MacLeod of Lewis

Opposite
Dunvegan Castle on the Isle of Skye has been the stronghold of the MacLeods for 700 years. The castle was impregnable because it could only be entered from the sea, so despite the disasters which overcame the MacLeods of Lewis in the 16th century, the MacLeods of Harris and of Dunvegan remained unchallenged.

The 15th Chief of the MacNab was taken prisoner by Jacobite forces after the battle of Prestonpans in 1745 and was confined in Doune Castle (pictured left).

MacMillan

MOTTO
Miseris succurrere disco
I learn to succour the unfortunate

The Gaelic name means 'son of the shaven-headed one' and the implication is that the founder was a monk (no doubt a high-flying abbot). However, MacMillans were to be found in many parts at a comparatively early date and it would be hard to prove that they shared a common ancestor. A substantial clan towards the end of the Middle Ages was MacMillan of Knap (Knapdale). They held a charter from the Lord of the Isles containing a promise, engraved on a rock by Loch Sween, that they should hold the land 'as long as the sea beats on the rock'. But the Campbells acquired Knapdale in the 18th century and, tradition says, Campbell of Cawdor threw the rock into the sea. There were also MacMillans in Lochaber, linked at first with the Mackintoshes, later with the Camerons of Lochiel, and in Strathclyde and Galloway. The well-known publishing family, which included a British prime minister, Harold Macmillan, held land in Arran and Strathclyde.

MacMillan

MacNab

MOTTO
Timor omnis abesto
Let fear be far from all

In the old Celtic Church, high offices were usually hereditary among leading families. Nor was marriage prohibited, so it is not surprising that many clans have an ecclesiastical ancestry. The MacNabs are 'sons of the abbot', possibly St. Fillan, abbot of Glendochart in the 7th century. Though their numbers were not

MacNab

large, the MacNabs were a fierce and independent breed, and their chiefs were men of forceful character, as is evident in Raeburn's great portrait of the 16th MacNab (1734-1816). A famous exploit of the MacNabs, in the course of their long feud with their MacNeish neighbours, was to carry a boat on a winter's night in 1612 from Loch Tay over the hills to Loch Earn (a feat scarcely to be believed had it not been duplicated by a group of Black Watch territorials in 1965). On their way back, the MacNabs were forced to abandon their boat in the hills as they were encumbered by bags containing the heads of the slaughtered MacNeishes. During the civil wars of the 17th century, the MacNabs fought for the King, with the result that their castle of Eilean Ran was destroyed and their lands taken over by the Campbells. They were regained after the Restoration (1660). They were less than enthusiastic Jacobites and in 1745 the MacNab adhered to the Government, and kept his lands. But the 16th Chief was the last of his line, and

the chiefship passed to a reprobate nephew who disappeared one day, to the consternation of his creditors, and later turned up in Canada where he tried to exploit immigrant MacNabs and ended up in the courts. The lands were sold to the Earl of Breadalbane (Campbell of Glenorchy). In the present century a small part was repurchased, and the current MacNab lives in Kinnel House, the home of his predecessors.

MacNaughton

MOTTO
I hoip in God

The MacNaughtons (variously spelled), were of Pictish stock and were probably resident in Strathtay before the main clan settled in Argyll, between Loch Fyne and Loch Awe, the future heartland of the Campbells. As followers of the MacDougall lords of Lorne, they supported Balliol against Bruce and suffered as a result, but largely regained their position in the 14th century when their headquarters were at Dunderave Castle on Loch Fyne. Their loyalty to the Stewart dynasty during the 17th century seems foolhardy in view of the proximity of the earls of Argyll, and the lands were lost after the 16th Laird of MacNaughton took arms with 'Bonnie Dundee' at Killiecrankie (1689). His successor planned to marry the prettier of the two daughters of Campbell of Ardkinglas in 1700 but drank so much before the wedding that he failed to notice that the uglier daughter had been substituted. He then eloped to Ireland with the

MacNaughton

pretty sister. Ardkinglas took over the forfeited lands and the chiefship languished for over a century until a descendant of Sir Alexander MacNaughton, who died at Flodden (1513), was discovered in County Antrim, and subsequently recognized as chief.

MacNeil

MOTTO
Buaidh no bas
To conquer or die

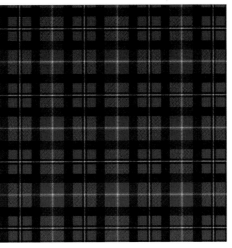

MacNeil

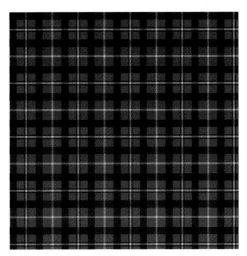

MacNeil of Barra

The MacNeils, or MacNeills, inhabited the smaller islands of the Hebrides and were certainly of common ancestry. The **MacNeils of Barra** claimed descent from the Irish High King, Niall of the Nine Hostages, who lived in the 4th century, but took their name from a later Irish Niall, who lived around 1300. The first documented MacNeil chief had a charter from the Lord of the Isles for Barra in 1427. The MacNeils of Barra were subjects of the Lord of the Isles, and after the collapse of the lordship lived largely by piracy, secure in their stronghold of Kisimul on a rocky island in Castle Bay. They were equally famous for their pride and their poverty. In the evening a

Below
Castle Bay, dominated by Kisimul Castle on the Isle of Barra, was the rocky stronghold of the MacNeils.

trumpeter blew his horn from the ramparts and declared that, since the great MacNeil of Barra had finished eating, the lesser princes of the world might now sit down to dine. The MacNeils of Barra were generally loyal to the Stewart dynasty and took part in the Jacobite risings in the 18th century. Barra was sold in 1838, but the chiefship later descended to an American, who repurchased much of Barra and restored Kisimul Castle.

The **MacNeills of Colonsay** (they generally preferred that spelling) were originally based in Knapdale and on Gigha, off Kintyre, which was sold in 1554 but regained from the Campbells a couple of generations later. The genealogy of the MacNeills is even more complicated than most clans, and there was a great deal of swapping of land between various branches. Colonsay and Oronsay, inhabited by the MacNeills since early times, were acquired by Donald MacNeil of Crear in Knapdale in 1700 in an exchange with the Campbells of Argyll. In the early 19th century, Colonsay, a fertile island, was reasonably prosperous thanks to the kelp industry and the efforts of the current chief, known as the Old Laird. But the good times did not last and Colonsay was sold off around the end of the century.

MacNeill of Colonsay

MacPherson

MOTTO
Touch not the cat but a glove

The name means 'son of the parson', and the McPhersons of Badenoch were rivals of the Mackintoshes, with whom they disputed the captaincy of Clan Chattan. That rivalry was exploited by a succession of powerful neighbours and overlords, the Comyns, the Stewarts, and finally the Gordon earls of Huntly. Although MacPherson of Cluny, the senior line, signed the Clan Chattan bond of union in 1609, the Clan generally showed little enthusiasm for making common cause with the Mackintosh. They were royalists during the civil wars of the 17th century, and Ewen of Cluny led the Badenoch forces under Montrose. Alexander MacPherson of Invereshie was a Jacobite agent after 1688, and the clan provided 600 men for Prince Charles Edward in the Forty-Five, when Ewen of Cluny gained a great reputation. He arrived too late to fight at Culloden and afterwards spent nine years in hiding in 'Cluny's Cage' on Ben Alder, before escaping to France. The confiscated estates were restored to his son, Cluny was rebuilt, and the chiefs maintained the old traditions in some style throughout the 19th century. Cluny was eventually sold in the 1930s. The Clan Museum at Newtonmore, opened in 1952, was the first of its kind. The MacPherson hunting tartan is probably one of the oldest authentic tartans. It is said to derive from the 'grey plaid of Badenoch' copied in 1745 by Lady Cluny-MacPherson from an old plaid at Cluny.

MacPherson

MacQuarrie

MOTTO
An t'arm breac dearg
The red tartaned army

The name comes from *guaire*, meaning 'noble' and according to tradition refers to a brother of Fingon, ancestor of the MacKinnons. Their plant badge features the pine tree, marking the MacQuarries as *Síol*

MacQuarrie

Alpin, kin of (Kenneth) MacAlpin. Their home was Ulva, off Mull, and they also held Staffa and land on Mull. They were loyal subjects of the Lords of the Isles, later of the royal Stewarts, but were never numerous. They became followers of MacLean of Duart, and were decimated in the battle of Inverkeithing (1651), when the chief and many clansmen were killed. In 1773, Samuel Johnson and James Boswell visited Ulva and were impressed by the intelligence of the chief, Lachlan MacQuarrie. A few years later he was forced to sell up and himself enlisted in the army (at the alleged age of 63). His cousin, also Lachlan MacQuarrie, was a respected governor of New South Wales (1810-1821) and, today, there are many more MacQuarries in Australia and North America than there are in Scotland.

Below
Fingal's Cave, Staffa, off the Isle of Mull, was held by the MacQuarrie. They also had land on Ulva and Mull.

MacRae

MOTTO
Fortitudine
With fortitude

*C*an MacRae is associated above all with Kintail and the castle of Eilean Donan, but not all MacRaes are related to the Highland clan. The name is one of many forms of the Gaelic *Mac Rath*, meaning 'son of grace', and is unlikely to have anything to do with a particular individual. The MacRaes lived originally near Inverness and were closely linked with the Frasers, but by 1400 they were established in Kintail, Wester Ross, attached to the rising power of the Mackenzies, whom they served as Constables of Eilean Donan castle among other offices. There are many stories of military feats performed by members of the clan that gained them the nickname, 'Mackenzies' shirt of mail'. During the abortive Jacobite rising of 1719 Spanish troops hired by the Mackenzie were billeted at Eilean Donan and the castle was afterwards blown up. It was lavishly restored in the 1930s and has become one of the commercial media's favourite images of the Highlands.

MacRae

Right
The MacRae were originally Constables of Eilean Donan Castle which was restored in the 1930s by one of their modern day descendants. It is now the most famous of Scotland's historic houses.

Matheson

MOTTO
Fac et spera
Do and hope

The name is not uncommon in Scotland, but not all Mathesons are related to the clan whose home was Lochalsh and who claimed descent from the same ancestor as the Mackenzies, Gilleon of the Aird. The Mathesons supported the Lord of the Isles, who also became Earl of Ross in the 15th century. According to one report, they were at that time on a more or less equal footing with their Mackenzie kin, but, weakened by adherence to the MacDonalds and by their own feuds, they failed to match the Mackenzie expansion. Mathesons as well as MacRaes were Constables of Eilean Donan castle for the Mackenzie. Iain Dubh defended the castle against MacDonald of Sleat in 1539 (both chiefs dying in the battle), and many branches of the Mathesons descended from his sons, including the Mathesons of the Black Isle who in later times inherited the chiefship. By the early 19th century virtually all the Mathesons' lands had been lost, but in the 1840s James Matheson and his nephew Alexander, two merchants of Highland origin who had made large fortunes in the Eastern trade, purchased the old homeland in Lochalsh as well as part of Lewis.

Matheson

Opposite
Caerlaverock Castle in lower Nithsdale was the stronghold of the Maxwell clan.

Maxwell

Maxwell

MOTTO
Reviresco
I grow strong again

The famous Border clan of Maxwell was probably of English origin. In the 13th century John of Maccuswell was Chamberlain of Scotland and at that time his family probably already held their famous stronghold of Caerlaverock, in lower Nithsdale. His immediate successors were the ancestors of numerous branches, which were apt to feud among themselves although, when kinship was reinforced by feudal obligations, the Maxwells of Caerlaverock were able to command substantial forces. The Maxwells benefited from the decline of the Black Douglases and from 1424 the chiefs held the title Lord Maxwell, frequently holding the office of wardens of the Western Marches. In general, they were inclined to co-operate with the royal government; locally, their chief rivals were the Johnstones and the violence between them continued into the 17th century, after the accession of James VI to the throne of England which ultimately transformed society in the Borders. The chiefs, earls of Nithsdale from the 17th century, embraced the Jacobite cause, and the 5th Earl was captured in the Fifteen. He was sentenced to death, but his mettlesome wife secured his escape from the Tower of London disguised as a maidservant, and they got away to Rome. Among many branches were the Maxwells of Monreith, who included Sir Herbert Maxwell (1845-1937) and his son Gavin (1914-1969), author of *Ring of Bright Water* (1960).

Menzies

MOTTO
Vil God I Zal

Usually pronounced Mingies, the name, which has several variants in Scotland, including Meyners, appears to be of Anglo-Norman origin and equivalent to the English Manners. It appeared first in Lothian, but the clan was established in Atholl in the 13th century and, after the success of Bruce, whom they supported, the Menzies collectively became one of the largest landholders in the southern Highlands. King James IV created a barony for Sir Robert Menzies, who was probably the original builder of Castle Weems, later called Castle Menzies. They were involved in various disputes over property with the Campbells, Stewarts of Garth and others, and the castle was destroyed in the early 16th century but soon rebuilt on the Z-plan, the culminating plan of the fortified house. Later expanded in Scots-Baronial style, it fell into ruin but was recently restored, in part, by the Clan Menzies Society. The Menzies were to be found on both sides of the religious and political conflicts of the 17th–18th centuries, the senior house of Weems tending towards the Protestant succession. A member of that family was also responsible for introducing the larch to the Highlands where it now seems so much at home.

Menzies

Moncreiffe

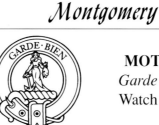

MOTTO
Sur esperance
Upon hope

Not many Scottish families have remained in the same home from the beginning of documentary records until now, but the Moncreiffes, whose name means 'hill of the sacred bough' (i.e. Moncreiffe Hill, near Perth), are one of the exceptions. The historian of the clans, Sir Iain Moncreiffe of that ilk, ascribed his family's survival to their loyalty to the royal government and avoidance of hazardous involvement in national affairs. The House of Moncreiffe was built in the late 17th century, replacing a medieval tower house, and was destroyed in a fire in 1957 in which the 23rd Laird lost his life. Parts were incorporated in the new building. The three main branches of the Moncreiffes can be distinguished by the spellings of their names. The Moncreiffs of Tulliebole dropped the final 'e'; other cadet branches are called Moncrieff. The Moncreiffes were associated with the Murrays of Atholl for centuries and wore their tartan until recent times, when the present Moncreiffe tartan, a simple diced sett of the kind that seems to have been common before tartans became emblems of identity, was designed by Sir Iain.

Moncreiffe

Opposite
Sir Andrew Murray was Wallace's chief lieutenant. He was killed at The Battle of Stirling Bridge in 1297.

Montgomery

MOTTO
Garde bien
Watch well

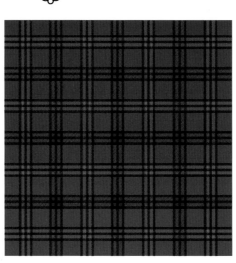

Montgomery

The first British Montgomery, or Montgomerie, came over with the Conqueror in 1066 and a (probable) grandson acquired Eaglesham, south of Glasgow, which his family retained until the 19th century. His descendants became lords Montgomery and, in 1507, earls of Eglinton. The 1st Earl held Brodick Castle and the Isle of Arran before the Hamiltons. The Montgomerys were involved in one of Scotland's longest-running feuds, with the Cunninghams. As so often, the original dispute was a minor one, but every time the matter appeared to have been settled, some new offence would reignite hostility. The 4th Earl was killed by the Cunninghams (1586) and Eglinton House destroyed. The death of the 5th Earl without an heir in 1612 finally ended the feud. His successor was Alexander Seton, a grandson of the 3rd Earl, who adopted his mother's name and was recognized as chief. In a later generation the earldom was inherited by another branch, and the 13th Earl acquired some fame for sponsoring the Eglinton Tournament in 1839, a Victorian pantomime of medieval jousting and feasting, rather spoiled by heavy rain.

Morrison

MOTTO
Teaghlach Phabbay
Pabbay family

The name appears in many regions in the era when surnames were coming into fashion, and it is unlikely that the source is the same in all cases. However, it was most common in the far north-west, and the Morrisons of the Outer Hebrides, who were renowned as poets and musicians, may well have descended from the Irish bards known as O'Muirgheasain, who settled in Mull in the 16th century. The name is also an anglicized version of *Mac Ghille Mhuire*, 'son of the servant of Mary'. In Lewis, Morrisons held the office of *britheamh* (brieve or hereditary judge) under the MacLeods and held land in the district of Ness. They were linked with the Mackenzies in some manner – Iain Dubh Morrison was killed by the MacLeods in the early 17th century – though the Morrisons resisted the Mackenzie takeover, which coincided with the disappearance of their hereditary office. There were also several branches of Clan Morrison in Harris, where they were smiths to MacLeod of Harris, and in Caithness, where they were linked with the Mackays. The Morrison tartan is identical to the Mackays' with the addition of a red line.

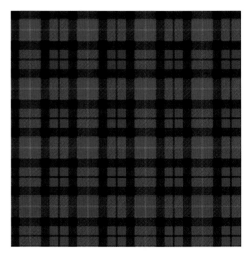

Morrison

Munro

MOTTO
Dread God

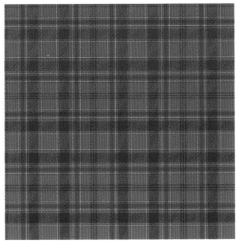

Munro

The Munros were established in the fertile district north of the Cromarty Firth, the chief resident in Foulis Castle, by the 14th century. Their earlier history is uncertain, though one theory traces the name to the River Roe in Northern Ireland. They were tenants of the earls of Ross, later the Crown, and fought in royal service, George Munro of Foulis falling in the Battle of Pinkie (1547). Renowned warriors, they became Protestants in the Reformation and, under Robert, 'the Black Baron', fought in the Thirty Years' War along with the Mackays. The Swedish army is said to have contained 27 officers of the rank of captain or above named Munro. The 18th Chief died of wounds, and a record of the campaign was compiled by Robert Munro of Obsdale, whose family inherited the chiefship in 1651 on the extinction of the original Foulis line. During the 17th-century civil wars, Munros fought on both sides, but they were strong supporters of the government against the Jacobites in the 18th century. The old castle of Foulis was destroyed by fire, but rebuilt by Sir Harry Munro (died 1781) in its present imposing form. Many distinguished men later bore the name. The U.S. president, James Monroe (1758-1831), is said to have descended from the Munros of Foulis.

Murray

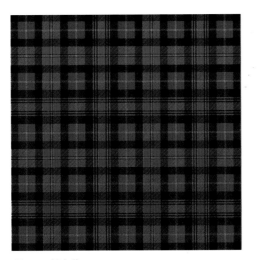

MOTTO
Furth fortune and fill the fetters

Moray was a Pictish kingdom in the early Middle Ages, and the Murrays (or Morays) were no doubt of Pictish descent, though their alleged ancestor, Freskin, may have been a Flemish adventurer. His grandson, William de Moravia, held lands in Moray from David II. He produced many successful offspring, who in turn founded further branches, so that landholding Murrays were to be found all over Scotland in the later Middle Ages. Clan spirit was necessarily diluted, but it existed: in the 16th century Murray chieftains came together to form a defensive pact and acknowledged Murray of Tullibardine as overall chief. The first to figure prominently in national history were Lowlanders, lords of Bothwell, who were prominent in the struggle for independence against the English. Sir Andrew Murray of Bothwell was Wallace's chief lieutenant and, some said, the better general. He was killed at Stirling Bridge (1297) and Wallace never won another battle. The Murrays of Tullibardine were probably descended from a younger son of William de Moravia. They held land in Strathearn and were created earls of Tullibardine in 1606. Their numerous cadet branches included the Murrays of Ochtertyre and the earls of Mansfield, whose seat was Scone Palace. An older branch were the Morays of Abercairney, founded by Sir John Murray of

Murray of Atholl

Bothwell, whose son became earl of Strathearn in the 14th century.

The most famous family is **Murray of Atholl**, descended from a younger son of the 2nd Earl of Tullibardine who married the heiress to the Stewart Earl of Atholl. His descendants became marquesses and, in 1703, dukes of Atholl. The 1st Duke was a vigorous opponent of the Act of Union (1707), but his successors supported the Government in the 18th century although the majority of Athollmen were Stewarts and thus favoured the Jacobites. Their leader in the Forty-Five was Lord George Murray, fifth son of the 1st Duke, who had fought in the Fifteen but rallied to the cause in 1745 with reluctance. He became Prince Charles Edward's leading general, though they fell out after Murray's insistence on a retreat from Derby. In one of the hard ironies of civil war, Lord George found himself besieging Blair Castle, his family seat, in 1746. The castle has since been considerably altered, and is now one of Scotland's most popular attractions. The Atholl Highlanders, once a formidable force, still exist as a ceremonial guard – the last private army in Britain. The Murray of Atholl tartan has a rather tenuous claim to antiquity, being said to resemble a Murray tartan worn in the 17th century.

Left
Blair Castle is the seat of the Murrays of Atholl. It has been considerably altered over the years and is now one of Scotland's most popular attractions.

Napier

MOTTO
Sans tache
Without stain

*F*amily tradition ascribes the origin of the Napiers to the old earls of Lennox, though that is hard to reconcile with the derivation of the name from 'naperer', the official in charge of the royal linen. John de Napier held land of the Earl of Dumbarton in the 13th century and a presumed descendant was governor of Edinburgh Castle in the 14th century. His son, a successful merchant, acquired Merchiston, and many of his successors died fighting for the Crown. John, 8th Laird of Merchiston, was Master of the Mint under James VI. A fierce opponent of Roman Catholicism, he is remembered as the inventor of logarithms. His son and grandson were zealous royalists during the 17th-century civil wars, but the direct line died out with the 11th Laird. Since then the name has been associated with an extraordinary number of soldiers: during the Napoleonic wars there were six British generals and one admiral called Napier.

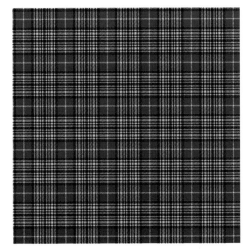

Napier

Nicolson (MacNicol)

MOTTO
Generositate
By generosity

The Nicolsons are associated with the north-west, Skye in particular, but the name appears frequently in Scotland at a comparatively early date and it is unlikely that all were connected. According to the old Celtic genealogies, the sons of Nicol originated in Assynt and Ullapool on the mainland, probably moving to Skye later, and eventually adopting the name Nicolson, rather than MacNicol (closer to the Gaelic). The chiefs held the land of Scorrybreac for many centuries and played a prominent part in the history of Skye, producing many bards and churchmen and a chronicler of the Hebrides (Donald MacNicol) in the late 17th century. They were still there in 1813, when Malcolm Nicolson of Scorrybreac died at the age of 86, but a later chief emigrated to Australia where there was, perhaps still is, a sheep station called Scorrybreac. The chiefship passed to a Lowland family, the Nicolsons of Lasswade.

Nicolson (MacNicol)

Opposite
Edinburgh Castle and the Ross Fountain.
The 1st Lord Oliphant was ambassador to
France and keeper of the castle.

Ogilvie

MOTTO
A fin
To the end

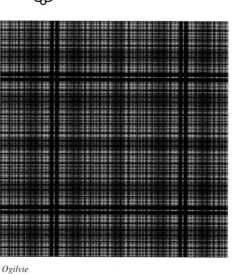
Ogilvie

The presumed founder of the Ogilvies of that ilk was Gillebride, or Gilbert, a son of the Earl (*Mormaer*) of Angus in the 12th century. He granted the lands of Ogilvie and Easter Powrie to his younger son, also Gilbert, and they were passed down in unbroken male descent for about 500 years. The chiefship, however, belonged to another branch, originally the Ogilvies of Auchterhouse, hereditary sheriffs of Angus in the 14th century. Sir Walter Ogilvie of Auchterhouse was killed at the Battle of Harlaw (1411). His younger son was Lord High Treasurer and the builder of the Tower of Airlie. A successor became Earl of Airlie in 1639 and was acknowledged as chief of the clan. Loyal supporters of the Stewart dynasty, the Ogilvies conducted ferocious feuds with their neighbours, the Lindsays, and later with the Campbells. The well-known ballad concerning the destruction of the 'bonnie house of Airlie' describes events during the Marquess of Argyll's campaign of 1640, which encouraged Montrose to intervene against him. The 2nd Earl of Airlie was captured at Philiphaugh (1645), the battle that ended Montrose's campaign. He later escaped from St. Andrew's Castle in the traditional manner, disguised as a woman. The Ogilvies were 'out' in the Jacobite risings, and a son of the 5th Earl led the men of Angus at Culloden. The title was restored to his descendants and the 8th Earl of

Airlie was killed in the South African War in 1900. His wife heard the ghostly drumming that always announces the death of an earl of Airlie. Another branch of the Ogilvies became earls of Findlater (1638) and of Seafield (1701), that title later passing to the lairds of Grant. The present chief still holds Airlie, but his seat is the handsome Cortachy Castle near Forfar. Angus Ogilvie, a younger son of the Earl of Airlie, married Princess Alexandra in 1963.

Oliphant

MOTTO
Tout pourvoir
Provide for all

The founder of the family was probably an Anglo-Norman lord who came north with David I and was granted land in the borders. Variants of the name are numerous, and some say that the present form resulted from tales of elephants brought back by Crusaders. Sir John Oliphant held Aberdalgie (near Perth) in the early 15th century, and his descendants played an important part in national affairs. His son Laurence, 1st Lord Oliphant, was ambassador to France and keeper of Edinburgh Castle. The 2nd Lord Oliphant died at Flodden (1513) and his grandson was captured at Solway Moss (1542). The 5th Lord Oliphant was involved in the Raid of Ruthven, a conspiracy backed by the English which involved the kidnapping of James VI. The family subsequently lost their lands, but a cadet branch, the Oliphants of nearby Gask survived. They were fanatical

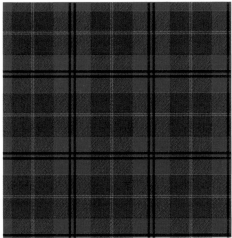

Oliphant

Jacobites. Carolina Oliphant (later Lady Nairne), born at Gask in 1766 and named after Prince Charles Edward, wrote the famous Jacobite songs, 'Charlie is my darling' and 'Will ye no come back again?'

Ramsay

MOTTO
Ora et labora
Pray and work

The origin of the name is uncertain, but it was probably a place in Lothian where Simon de Ramsay held land in the 12th century. A presumed descendant held Dalhousie by 1300. He was active against the English, as was his son, Alexander, who, however, fell foul of Sir William Douglas (the Knight of Liddesdale) and is said to have died of starvation in Hermitage Castle. Nevertheless, the Ramsays of Dalhousie prospered and founded several cadet branches. One of these, the Ramsays of Melrose, became earls of Dalhousie in the 17th century. The last of their line was the Marquess of Dalhousie, who became Governor General of India in 1847 at the age of 34.

Ramsay

Opposite
Drumlarig Castle, one of three of the Scott family's great houses.

Robertson

MOTTO
Virtutis gloria merces
Glory is the reward

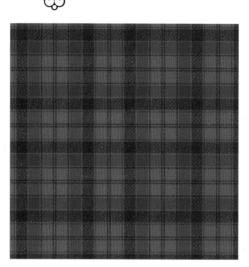

Robertson

The Robertsons are *Clann Donnchaidh*, 'children of Duncan'. He was an early 14th-century chief who was himself descended from the old earls of Atholl, and they were descended from King Duncan, who was a son of Abbot Crinan of Dunkeld, guardian of the relics of St. Columba. This inheritance, long claimed by the Robertsons, is no longer disputed. Duncan's grandson was Robert, from whom most of the clan took their name (others took different names, such as Duncanson), and he received the barony of Struan, the origin of the name by which the chiefs have been known since the 16th century, Struan Robertson. The Robertsons were loyal supporters of the Stewart dynasty, but in their beautiful Atholl homeland they suffered from the proximity of powerful neighbours, the Stewarts of Atholl, the Murrays and the Campbells. They were loyal supporters of the Stewart monarchy – their crest is a hand supporting a crown – and the 17th Struan Robertson had the remarkable record of taking part in virtually every Jacobite rising between 1689 and 1745, in spite of imprisonment, exile, loss of his lands and other disincentives. The Robertson lands, already much diminished, were forfeit in 1746, though some were later regained. The last of the land in Rannoch was sold in the early 20th century, and the chiefship moved abroad. The Clan museum near Blair Atholl contains many interesting relics, including the magic stone, *Clach na Brataich*, which figures in clan legend since the time of Duncan Reamhar, 'the Stout', who fought with Bruce at Bannockburn.

Rose

MOTTO
Constant and true

The Roses of Kilravock, near Cawdor, can be traced back to the early 13th century, and are thought to be of Norman origin. Ros in Normandy is a possible source of the name. The chiefs of Rose, generally named Hugh, were lords of Kilravock for about 600 years, succession usually passing from father to son. The family history suggests that it was possible for Highland lairds to live in relative peace with their neighbours. Asked by James VI how he managed it, the 10th Rose of Kilravock, known as the Black Baron, replied that he prayed three times a day instead of once. Kilravock Castle, recently the scene of international clan gatherings, was never sacked. It still retains parts of the medieval structure and contains almost unrivalled family archives. But feuds were not entirely avoided. There was trouble with Dunbars, Urquharts and Mackenzies, as well as a famous conflict with Campbell of Cawdor over an abducted heiress. Nor could the Roses always avoid national disturbances. Kilravock opposed the union with England (1707) but remained more or less neutral during the Jacobite risings when Roses were to be found on both sides. Before Culloden (fought

Rose

nearby), Rose of Kilravock entertained Prince Charles Edward and the Duke of Cumberland on successive evenings.

Ross

MOTTO
Spem successus alit
Success nourishes hope

Ross

The Rosses claim descent from the old Celtic earls of Ross who, in turn, were probably descended from the Irish High King, Niall of the Nine Hostages. Their homeland was the peninsula of Easter Ross, north of the Cromarty Firth, a fertile land not immediately threatened by land-hungry neighbours. The 4th Earl of Ross married a sister of Robert Bruce and was killed in battle in 1333 even though he was wearing the sacred shirt of St. Duthac, supposed to ensure impregnability. The 5th Earl died without a male heir which resulted in the conflict over the earldom between the Lord of the Isles and the Regent Albany and the bloody Battle of Harlaw (1411). The chiefship (not the earldom) subsequently passed to the Rosses of Balnagowan. Their situation kept the Rosses comparatively remote from national politics, and little is known of events in succeeding centuries, except for occasional outbreaks of violence. A 16th-century chief, Alexander of Balnagowan, was such a reprehensible leader that his own son was commissioned to proceed against him with fire and sword and the last effective Balnagowan chief was another bad hat. After his death in the late 17th century, the estates passed to a Lowland family which, though named Ross, was completely unrelated to the clan. The chiefship was exercised unofficially by the cadet branch of Pitcalnie, who did not become chiefs in fact until the present century. Soon afterwards, the chiefship passed to another cadet branch, Ross of Shandwick.

Scott

MOTTO
Amo
I love

The Scotts can be traced back to the 12th century, and the founder of the senior family, the Scotts of Buccleuch, was Richard le Scot, whose estates in Lanark were the basis for the considerable holdings of his decendants. They acquired Branxholm, still the seat of the dukes of Buccleuch, in the 14th century. As a large Border clan, the Scotts came into their own after the eclipse of the Douglases in 1455. Their enemies included, besides the English (who burned Branxholm Castle more than once), the Kerrs, one or other usually being warden of the Middle March. The 1st Lord Scott of Buccleuch, created 1606, was leader of a famous raid on Carlisle gaol (1596) to rescue an Armstrong chieftain. His son became 1st Earl of Buccleuch, and the 2nd Earl was succeeded by his son-in-law, the bastard son of Charles II who took the name Scott and became Duke of Monmouth. After his botched rebellion and execution, his wife, the 2nd Earl's daughter, became duchess in her own right and the title and lands were passed down from her. The 3rd Duke married the heiress of the (Douglas) Duke of Queensberry and became one of the richest men in Britain. The novelist Sir Walter Scott (1771-1832), who did more for his country's image than perhaps any other person in history, belonged to a junior branch, the Scotts of Harden.

Scott

Abbotsford, country home of Sir Walter Scott in the country near Montrose, Angus. The splendid Gothic-style house is still inhabited by Scott's descendants.

Sinclair

MOTTO
Commit thy work to God

The name is of Norman origin, and Henry de Saint-Clair held lands in Lothian in the 12th century. His successors became prominent in national affairs: one fought at Bannockburn, another died on crusade with Douglas in Spain. The son of the latter married the heiress of Orkney and Caithness, and their son became Earl of Orkney, the senior member of the Norwegian nobility, in 1379. He also maintained a considerable fleet engaged in piracy. The Orkney title lasted only two generations after him, but the earldom of Caithness was later restored and is still held. The grim and gaunt ruins of Girnigo Castle, rising sheer from sea-girt cliffs north of Wick, is a suitable symbol of the violence that encompassed the Sinclairs. The 4th Earl kept his eldest son in chains for seven years; hastening his death by denying him water, and there were many relentless blood feuds. Most of the lands were eventually lost to the Gordons and others. Among distinguished cadet branches were the Sinclairs of Ulbster. They included the agricultural reformer and authority on Highland custom, Sir John Sinclair of Ulbster (1754-1835), whose portrait by Raeburn is one of the glories of the National Portrait Gallery in Edinburgh.

Sinclair

Skene

MOTTO
Virtutis regia merces
A palace the reward of bravery

A 'skene' (*sgian*) is a knife or dagger, and legend relates how the progenitor of the Skenes saved the life of the king by stabbing a wolf with such a weapon. The Skenes were a sept of Clan Donnchaidh, most of whom later

100

took the name Robertson, and the barony of Skene, west of Aberdeen, may have been named after its holders rather than, as usual, vice versa. The barony was confirmed by a charter of Bruce in 1318, and the clan, though small, appears to have prospered. Provost Skene's house in Aberdeen, now a museum, was acquired by George Skene in the 17th century. When the last of the lairds of Skene died childless in 1827, the lands passed to a nephew, the Earl of Fife, and the chiefship to an emigrant branch. William Forbes Skene, a great authority on Celtic Scotland in the 19th century, sprang from a cadet branch, the Skenes of Rubislaw.

Skene

Stewart

*W*alter FitzAlan, whose ancestors were Bretons rather than Normans (and therefore Celts), came north with David I in 1124. He was appointed to the office of High Steward, which became hereditary in his family and gave them their surname, Stewart. (The form 'Stuart' became common in the 16th century and is usually applied to the dynasty after James VI became James I of England.) The 6th High Steward married Bruce's daughter Marjorie, and when King David II died childless in 1371, their son became the first of the royal dynasty as Robert II. The history of that dynasty is, of course, part of the history not only of Scotland but of Great Britain and

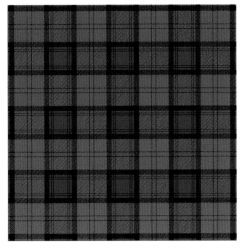

Stewart

Ireland. The last of the line was Henry, Cardinal York, brother of Prince Charles Edward ('Bonnie Prince Charlie'), who died in 1788. Paradoxically, representation of the Stewart line then passed to George III, as a descendant of James VI and I. That was recognized by Cardinal York who left what remnants he possessed of Scottish regalia to George III and his descendants. The Royal Stewart tartan is said to have been worn by George IV on his famous visit to Scotland in 1822. Romantic supposition has linked it with Prince Charles Edward in 1745, but there is little evidence of its existence much before 1822. It has become the most popular of Scottish tartans but is in fact never worn by royalty.

It is said that not all Stewarts are kin to the king, but a great many were. Stewarts at one time held more than 20 titles of the rank of earl or above, and many lesser ones, and most if not all could trace their ancestry to Sir John Stewart of Bonkyl, a son of the 4th Steward and grandfather of the first Stewart king. The **Stewarts of Atholl** became prominent during that reign. One of Robert II's sons was made

Stewart of Atholl

Earl of Buchan, though was better known as the infamous 'Wolf of Badenoch', a ferocious bandit with a host of illegitimate sons as vicious as himself. On his death, the earldom passed to his brother, the Duke of Albany, whose descendants included the Stewarts of Ardvorlich and the earls of Moray. The Stewarts of Garth, perhaps the most famous branch of the Atholl Stewarts, were descended from one of the Wolf's sons. In 1437 the widow of King James I married another decendant of Sir John Stewart of Bonkyl, and their son was given the title of Earl of Atholl by James II, his half-brother. Atholl had formerly been held by the royal line, and it reverted to the Crown on the death of the 5th Earl in 1595, but in 1625 passed to the Earl of Tullibardine, a Murray. The Stewarts of Atholl remained among the

Stewart of Appin

most fervent supporters of the royal line, but their overlords, the Murrays, were less enthusiastic. However, the Atholl Stewarts served the cause under their own commanders. In 1689 they rallied to 'Bonnie Dundee' (Graham of Claverhouse) under Stewart of Ballechin, a family descended from an illegitimate son of James II.

Several notable families, including the **Stewarts of Appin** who formed a self-contained west Highland clan, traced their descent from Sir James Stewart of Pirston (Pearston), a younger son of the productive Sir John Stewart of Bonkyl. Dugald, the first Stewart of Appin, was five generations removed from Sir James of Pirston and was himself the founder of several cadet branches. Like other Stewarts, the Stewarts of Appin were loyal supporters of their remote royal relations. After taking part in Montrose's campaign of 1645, they signed a bond of association with the

Dunrobin Castle, the seat of the Sutherland clan, was transformed from a Scottish castle into a French château by Sir Charles Barry.

Stewarts of Atholl and other branches. They were 'out' again in 1689 with 'Bonnie Dundee', when they were led by the chief of a cadet branch, Stewart of Ardshiel, the Appin chief being a minor. A similar situation arose in 1745, but the Stewarts of Appin suffered no less than others in the campaign against the clans after Culloden. A famous episode, the Appin Murder, when a brother of the chief was convicted and executed for murdering a Campbell (though he was not the offender) after a trial presided over by the Duke of Argyll, is remembered through Robert Louis Stevenson's account in *Kidnapped*.

A descendant of another son of Sir John Stewart of Bonkyl was Sir John Stewart of Darnley (died 1429), who married a daughter of the Earl of Lennox. As a result, his grandson later inherited the earldom. The 4th Stewart Earl of Lennox (died 1571), was the father of Lord Darnley, who married Mary, Queen of Scots (his cousin), and fathered the future James VI before being blown up in his house near Edinburgh (he proved to have been strangled before the explosion). His father, the Earl, became one of Mary's fiercest oppponents. The Earl's granddaughter was Lady Arabella Stuart, the unfortunate object of various conspiracies over the succession, who died insane in the Tower of London in 1615, and his nephew was Esmé Stewart, adored by James VI who made him Duke of Lennox in 1581. The 2nd Duke also became Duke of Richmond and a thorough Englishman. The wife of the 6th Duke of Lennox, herself a Stewart, was the model for Britannia on the old

Sutherland

MOTTO
Sans peur
Without fear

The name is Norse, and Sutherland is one of the oldest continuous earldoms in the United Kingdom, created in the early 13th century. The 1st Earl was a descendant of William de Moravia, ancestor of the Murrays, and when surnames came to be generally adopted many Sutherland men took the name Murray. The earls were supporters of Bruce and the 5th Earl's son by a daughter of Bruce might have pre-empted the Stewart succession had he not died young. A daughter of the 9th Earl married Gordon of Aboyne, brother of the Earl of Huntly, and when he died, Gordon took possession of the earldom, successfully resisting the efforts of Elizabeth's half-brother, Alexander, to turn him out of the Sutherland stronghold of Dunrobin (today an imposing Victorian pile). The line of Gordon earls failed in 1766, and a great battle began, fought now with writs rather than claymores. The Gordons were again victorious, the late Earl's daughter becoming Countess of Sutherland in her own

Sutherland

right. She and her wealthy English husband, George Leveson-Gower, Marquess of Stafford, later became Duke and Duchess of Sutherland. They are remembered for the notorious Sutherland Clearances of the late 18th century. The Duke believed his expulsion of his tenants would prove beneficial to them, forcing them to move from the primitive conditions in which they lived. He had no sympathy with local culture, and the result was the final destruction of the clan. The 3rd Duke was a similar sort, investing heavily in the Highland railway but insisting it should take a roundabout route that would not interfere with the shooting. Among notable cadet houses were the Sutherlands of Forse and the Sutherlands of Duffus. Kenneth, Lord Duffus, fled abroad after the Fifteen and served in the Russian navy before marrying a Swedish noblewoman. Duffus was later restored to his grandson.

Thomson (MacThomas)

MOTTO
Deo juvante invidiam superabo
I will overcome envy with God's help

This is quite a common name in Scotland, an alternative form of the original Gaelic being MacTavish, the name of a sept of the Campbells of Argyll. Some of them were called Taweson, as well as Thomson, and they may have been related to the Border family, Thomson of that ilk. A sept of the MacFarlanes was descended from a younger son of an early MacFarlane chief named Thomas, and a larger group was a sept of Clan Chattan, resident in

Glenshee and Glenisla and descended from an illegitimate son of the 7th Mackenzie chief. Their name was most commonly anglicized as MacThomas and the name also appeared in the Isles. In Shetland, the usual spelling was Thomasson.

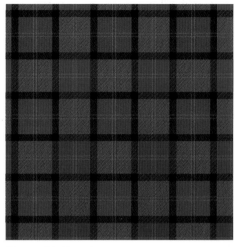

Thomson (MacThomas)

Urquhart

MOTTO
Meane weil speak weil and doe weil

Tradition links the Urquharts with Clan Forbes, and at one time they controlled most of the Black Isle. The name appears to derive from a topographical term, but there are several possibilities in Gaelic. The researches of the scholarly but eccentric Sir Thomas Urquhart of Cromarty (who died in 1660 of joy, it is said, at the Restoration of Charles II) traced Urquhart ancestry to the time of the pyramids, but the

Urquhart

first known to history lived in the 14th century, when the Urquharts gained the office of hereditary sheriffs of Cromarty. Other branches were established in Moray and Aberdeenshire and elsewhere. Sir Thomas Urquhart's activities on behalf of the Royalists in the 17th-century civil wars earned him two years in the Tower of London, where he embarked on the translation of Rabelais for which he is chiefly remembered. After his death the lands passed to a cousin, John Urquhart of Craigston, who sold them. Another branch of the family later regained them for a time in the 18th century. Castle Urquhart on Loch Ness was held only briefly by the Urquharts, but the Urquharts of Craigston still hold Castle Craig, or what remains of it, on the Cromarty Firth.

Wallace

MOTTO
Pro libertate
For liberty

Richard Wallensis (meaning 'the Welshman', in this case a man of the ancient British kingdom of Strathclyde) was a vassal of Walter the Steward, ancestor of the Stewarts, with lands at Richardston (Riccarton), south of Kilmarnock. His grandson, Adam Wallace of Riccarton, had two sons, the younger of whom received lands at Elderslie, near Paisley. There, William Wallace, the great national hero, was born in about 1275. After a private quarrel had led to his being outlawed, he became leader of resistance to the English in 1297, in the period when Edward I had conquered Scotland and imprisoned John Balliol, who had proved insufficiently subservient as king. At Stirling Bridge, Wallace and Sir Andrew Moray destroyed a large English army and freed most of Scotland. In the following year, Wallace was heavily defeated, but for seven years he remained at large, launching guerrilla attacks on the English. Captured in 1305, he was executed with appalling barbarity in London, in spite of the fact that, unlike most Scottish landholders, he had never sworn fealty to the English king and could in no sense be classed a traitor. Wallace left no known descendants, but many families are descended from the Wallaces of Riccarton.

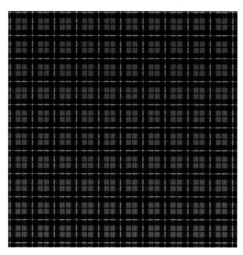

Wallace

Wemyss

MOTTO
Je pense
I think

Wemyss

The lands of Wemyss, in the Kingdom of Fife, were granted to a younger son of the (MacDuff) Earl of Fife in the early 12th century. The name may originally have been a corruption of the Gaelic word for 'cave', an interpretation encouraged by the presence of caves, containing Pictish inscriptions, below the ancient ruins of MacDuff's Castle in East Wemyss on the Firth of Forth. There were many branches of the family, but Wemyss of Wemyss was acknowledged as the senior line and the 5th Earl of Wemyss was officially acknowledged as representative of the family of the MacDuff earls of Fife and thus chief of the clan. His son, Lord Elcho, raised troops for Prince Charles Edward in the Forty-Five and died in exile. As

a result the chiefship and the title became permanently separated, one of Lord Elcho's brothers, who had adopted the name Charteris on inheriting a handsome legacy, gaining the title and the younger brother, James, becoming chief, with his seat at the castle of East Wemyss.

Scottish Family Names and their Associated Clans

There are endless variations in the spelling of Scottish surnames and many have possible links to particular clans mentioned in this book. This is by no means a comprehensive list.

Surname	Clan	Surname	Clan	Surname	Clan
ABBOT	MACNAB	BRYCE	MACFARLANE	COUTTS	FARQUHARSON
ABBOTSON	MACNAB	BUNTAIN	GRAHAM	COWAN	COLQUHOUN,
ADDISON	GORDON	BUNTEN	GRAHAM		MACDOUGALL
ADIE	GORDON	BUNTINE	GRAHAM	COWIE	FRASER
AIRLIE	OGILVIE	BURDON	LAMONT	CRERAR	MACKINTOSH
AICHESON	GORDON	BURKE	MACDONALD	CROMBIE	MACDONALD
AITKEN	GORDON	BURNES	CAMPBELL	CROOKSHANKS	STEWART
ALEXANDER	MACALISTER,	BURNS	CAMPBELL	CRUICKSHANK	STEWART
	MACDONALD	CADELL	CAMPBELL	CRUM	MACDONALD
ALISTAIR	MACALISTER	CAIRD	SINCLAIR,	CULLEN	GORDON
ALLAN	MACDONALD,		MACGREGOR	CUMIN	CUMMING
	MACFARLANE	CARISTON	SKENE	DALLAS	MACKINTOSH
ALLANSON	MACDONALD,	CARLYLE	BRUCE	DANIELS	MACDONALD
	MACFARLANE	CARR	KERR	DAVIS	DAVIDSON
ALLISON	MACALISTER	CARRICK	KENNEDY	DAWSON	DAVIDSON
ARROL	HAY	CARSON	MACPHERSON	DAY	DAVIDSON
ARTHUR	MACARTHUR	CASSELS	KENNEDY	DEAN	DAVIDSON
ASKEY	MACLEOD	CATTANACH	MACPHERSON	DENOON	CAMPBELL
AUSTIN	KEITH	CAW	MACFARLANE	DEUCHAR	LINDSAY
AYSON	MACKINTOSH	CESSFORD	KERR	DICKSON	KEITH
BAIN	MACBEAN,	CHARLES	MACKENZIE	DINGWALL	MUNRO,
	MACKAY	CHRISTIE	FARQUHARSON		ROSS
BALLOCH	MACDONALD	CLANACHAN	MACLEAN	DINNES	INNES
BARRIE	FARQUHARSON,	CLARK	CAMERON,	DIS	SKENE
	GORDON		MACPHERSON	DIXON	KEITH
BARRON	ROSE	CLARKE	CAMERON,	DOBBIE	ROBERTSON
BARTHOLOMEW	MACFARLANE,		MACPHERSON	DOBSON	ROBERTSON
	LESLIE	CLARKSON	CAMERON,	DOCHART	MACGREGOR
BEAN	MACBEAN		MACPHERSON	DOCHARTY	MACGREGOR
BEATH	MACDONALD,	CLEMENT	LAMONT	DOIG	DRUMMOND
	MACLEAN	CLERK	CAMERON,	DOLES	MACKINTOSH
BEATTIE	MACBEAN		MACPHERSON	DONACHIE	ROBERTSON
BEGG	MACDONALD	CLUNY	MACPHERSON	DONALDSON	MACDONALD
BERRY	FORBES	CLYNE	SINCLAIR	DONILLSON	MACDONALD
BETON	MACLEOD	COBB	LINDSAY	DONLEAVY	BUCHANAN
BINNIE	MACBEAN	COLLIER	ROBERTSON	DONLEVY	BUCHANAN
BLACK	LAMONT,	COLMAN	BUCHANAN	DONNELLSON	MACDONNELL
	MACGREGOR,	COLSON	MACDONALD	DOVE	BUCHANAN
	MACLEAN	COLYEAR	ROBERTSON	DOW	BUCHANAN,
BLAKE	LAMONT	COMBIE	THOMSON		DAVIDSON
BONAR	GRAHAM	COMINE	CUMMING	DOWE	BUCHANAN
BONTINE	GRAHAM	COMRIE	MACGREGOR	DOWNIE	LINDSAY
BOWERS	MACGREGOR	CONACHER	MACDOUGALL	DRYSDALE	DOUGLAS
BOWIE	MACDONALD	CONNELL	MACDONALD	DUFF	MACDUFF
BOWMAKER	MACGREGOR	CONOCHIE	CAMPBELL	DUFFUS	SUTHERLAND
BOWMAN	FARQUHARSON	CONSTABLE	HAY	DUILACH	STEWART
BOYES	FORBES	COOK	STEWART	DUNCANSON	ROBERTSON
BREBNER	FARQUHARSON	CORBET	ROSS	DUNNACHIE	ROBERTSON
BREWER	DUMMOND,	CORMACK	BUCHANAN	DUTHIE	ROSS
	MACGREGOR	COULL	MACDONALD	DYCE	SKENE
BROWN	LAMONT,	COULSON	MACDONALD	EADIE	GORDON
	MACMILLAN	COUSLAND	BUCHANAN	EATON	HOME

Scottish Family Names and their Associated Clans

Surname	Clan	Surname	Clan	Surname	Clan
EDIE	GORDON	HADDON	GRAHAM	LAWRENCE	MACLAREN
ELDER	MACKINTOSH	HAGGART	ROSS	LAWRIE	MACLAREN
ENNIS	INNES	HALLYARD	SKENE	LAWSON	MACLAREN
ENRICK	GUNN	HARDIE	FARQUHARSON,	LEAN	MACLEAN
ESSON	MACKINTOSH		MACKINTOSH	LECKIE	MACGREGOR
EWING	MACLACHLAN	HARDY	FARQUHARSON,	LECKY	MACGREGOR
FAIR	ROSS		MACKINTOSH	LEES	MACPHERSON
FAIRBAIRN	ARMSTRONG	HAROLD	MACLEOD	LEITCH	MACDONALD
FEDERITH	SUTHERLAND	HARPER	BUCHANAN	LEMOND	LAMONT
FERGUS	FERGUSSON	HARPERSON	BUCHANAN	LENNIE	BUCHANAN
FERRIES	FERGUSSON	HARVEY	KEITH	LEWIS	MACLEOD
FERSON	MACPHERSON	HASTINGS	CAMPBELL	LIMOND	LAMONT
FIFE	MACDUFF	HAWES	CAMPBELL	LIMONT	LAMONT
FINDLATER	OGILVIE	HAWSON	CAMPBELL	LINKLATER	SINCLAIR
FINDLAY	FARQUHARSON	HAWTHORN	MACDONALD	LOBBAN	LOGAN
FINDLAYSON	FARQUHARSON	HENDRIE	MACNAUGHTON	LOCKERBIE	DOUGLAS
FINLAYSON	FARQUHARSON	HENDRY	MACNAUGHTON	LOMBARD	STEWART,
FISHER	CAMPBELL	HEWITSON	MACDONALD	LONIE	CAMERON
FOULIS	MUNRO	HEWITT	MACDONALD	LORNE	STEWART,
FRANCE	STEWART	HIGGINSON	MACKINTOSH		CAMPBELL
FRANCIS	STEWART	HOBSON	ROBERTSON	LOUDOUN	CAMPBELL
FREW	FRASER	HOSSACK	MACKINTOSH	LOW	MACLAREN
FRISSELL	FRASER	HOWE	GRAHAM	LOWSON	MACLAREN
FRIZELL	FRASER	HOWIE	GRAHAM	LUCAS	LAMONT
FYFE	MACDUFF	HOWISON	MACDONALD	LUKE	LAMONT
GALLIE	GUNN	HUDSON	MACDONALD	LYALL	SINCLAIR
GALT	MACDONALD	HUGHSON	MACDONALD	MACA'CHALLIES	MACDONALD
GARROW	STEWART	HUNTLY	GORDON	MACACHOUNICH	COLQUHOUN
GARVIE	MACLEAN	HUTCHENSON	MACDONALD	MACADAM	MACGREGOR
GAUNSON	GUNN	HUTCHINSON	MACDONALD	MACADIE	FERGUSSON
GEDDES	GORDON	HUTCHISON	MACDONALD	MACAINDRA	MACFARLANE
GEORGESON	GUNN	INCHES	ROBERTSON	MACALDONICH	BUCHANAN
GIBB	BUCHANAN	INGRAM	COLQUHOUN	MACALDUIE	LAMONT
GIFFORD	HAY	INNIE	INNES	MACALLAN	MACDONALD,
GILBERT	BUCHANAN	ISLES	MACDONALD		MACFARLANE
GILBERTSON	BUCHANAN	JAMESON	GUNN,	MACALONIE	CAMERON
GILBRIDE	MACDONALD		STEWART	MACANDEOIR	BUCHANAN,
GILCHRIST	MACLACHLAN,	JAMIESON	GUNN,		MACNAB
	OGILVIE		STEWART	MACANDREW	MACKINTOSH
GILFILLAN	MACNAB	JEFFREY	MACDONALD	MACANGUS	MACINNES
GILL	MACDONALD	KAY	DAVIDSON	MACARA	MACGREGOR,
GILLANDERS	ROSS	KEAN	GUNN,		MACRAE
GILLESPIE	MACPHERSON		MACDONALD	MACAREE	MACGREGOR
GILLIES	MACPHERSON	KEENE	GUNN,	MACASKILL	MACLEOD
GILLON	MACLEAN		MACDONALD	MACASLAN	BUCHANAN
GILROY	GRANT,	KELLIE	MACDONALD	MACAUSELAN	BUCHANAN
	MACGILLIVRAY	KENDRICK	MACNAUGHTON	MACAUSLAN	BUCHANAN
GLENNIE	MACKINTOSH	KENNETH	MACKENZIE	MACAUSLAND	BUCHANAN
GORRIE	MACDONALD	KENNETHSON	MACKENZIE	MACAUSLANE	BUCHANAN
GOUDIE	MACPHERSON	KERRACHER	FARQUHARSON	MACBAXTER	MACMILLAN
GOW	MACPHERSON	KILGOUR	MACDUFF		MACDONALD,
GOWAN	MACDONALD	KING	COLQUHOUN		MACLEAN
GOWRIE	MACDONALD	KINNELL	MACDONALD	MACBEOLAIN	MACKENZIE
GREENLAW	HOME	KINNIESON	MACFARLANE	MACBETH	MACBEAN,
GREGORSON	MACGREGOR	KNOX	MACFARLANE		MACDONALD,
GREGORY	MACGREGOR	LACHIE	MACLACHLAN		MACLEAN
GREIG	MACGREGOR	LAIDLAW	SCOTT	MACBHEATH	MACBEAN,
GREUSACH	FARQUHARSON	LAIR	MACLAREN		MACDONALD,
GREWAR	MACGREGOR,	LAMB	LAMONT		MACLEAN
	DRUMMOND	LAMBIE	LAMONT	MACBRIDE	MACDONALD
GRIER	MACGREGOR	LAMMOND	LAMONT	MACBRIEVE	MORRISON
GRIESCK	MACFARLANE	LAMONDSON	LAMONT	MACBURIE	MACDONALD
GRIGOR	MACGREGOR	LANDERS	LAMONT	MACCAA	MACFARLANE
GRUAMACH	MACFARLANE	LANG	LESLIE	MACCABE	MACLEOD
GRUER	MACGREGOR,	LANSDALE	HOME	MACCAIG	FARQUHARSON,
	DRUMMOND	LAUCHLAN	MACLACHLAN		MACLEOD

Scottish Family Names and their Associated Clans

Surname	Clan	Surname	Clan	Surname	Clan
MACAISHE	MACDONALD	MACCRINDLE	MACDONALD	MACGOUN	MACDONALD,
MACCALL	MACDONALD	MACCRIRIE	MACDONALD		MACPHERSON
MACCALMAN	BUCHANAN	MACCROUTHER	MACGREGOR,	MACGOWAN	MACDONALD,
MACCALMONT	BUCHANAN		DRUMMOND		MACPHERSON
MACCAMIE	STEWART	MACCRUITHEIN	MACDONALD	MACGOWN	MACDONALD,
MACCAMMON	BUCHANAN	MACCUAG	MACDONALD		MACPHERSON
MACCAMMOND	BUCHANAN	MACCUAIG	FARQUHARSON,	MACGRATH	MACRAE
MACCANISH	MACINNES		MACLEOD	MACGREUSICH	BUCHANAN
MACANSH	MACINNES	MACCUBBIN	BUCHANAN		MACFARLANE
MACCARTNEY	FARQUHARSON,	MACCUISH	MACDONALD	MACGREWAR	MACGREGOR,
	MACKINTOSH	MACCUNE	MACEWAN		DRUMMOND
MACCARTAIR	CAMPBELL	MACCUNN	MACPHERSON	MACGRIME	GRAHAM
MACCARTER	CAMPBELL	MACCURRACH	MACPHERSON	MACGRORY	MACLAREN
MACCASH	MACDONALD	MACCUTCHEN	MACDONALD	MACGROWTHER	MACGREGOR,
MACCASKILL	MACLEOD	MACCUTCHEON	MACDONALD		DRUMMOND
MACCASLAND	BUCHANAN	MACDADE	DAVIDSON	MACGUARAN	MACQUARRIE
MACCAUL	MACDONALD	MACDAID	DAVIDSON	MACGUGAN	MACNEIL
MACCAUSE	MACFARLANE	MACDANIELL	MACDONALD	MACGUIRE	MACQUARRIE
MACCAW	MACFARLANE	MACDAVID	DAVIDSON	MACHARDIE	FARQUHARSON,
MACCAY	MACKAY	MACDERMID	CAMPBELL		MACKINTOSH
MACCEALLAICH	MACDONALD	MACDIARMID	CAMPBELL	MACHARDY	FARQUHARSON,
MACCHLERICH	CAMERON	MACDONACHIE	ROBERTSON		MACKINTOSH
MACCHLERY	CAMERON	MACDONLEAVY	BUCHANAN	MACHAROLD	MACLEOD
MACCHOITER	MACGREGOR	MACDRAIN	MACDONALD	MACHENDRIE	MACNAUGHTON
MACCHRUITER	BUCHANAN	MACDOUGALL	MACDOUGALL	MACHENDRY	MACNAUGHTON,
MACCLOY	STEWART	MACEACHAN	MACDONALD		MACDONALD
MACLURE	MACLEOD		OF CLAN RANALD	MACHOWELL	MACDOUGALL
MACCLUSKIE	MACDONALD	MACEACHERN	MACDONALD	MACHUGH	MACDONALD
MACCLYMONT	LAMONT	MACEACHRAN	MACDONALD	MACHUTCHEN	MACDONALD
MACCODRUM	MACDONALD	MACEARACHER	FARQUHARSON	MACIAN	GUNN,
MACCOLL	MACDONALD	MACELFRISH	MACDONALD		MACDONALD
MACCOLMAN	BUCHANAN	MACELHERAN	MACDONALD	MACILDOWIE	CAMERON
MACCOMAS	THOMSON	MACEOIN	MACFARLANE	MACILDUY	MACGREGOR,
MACCOMBE	THOMSON	MACEOL	MACNAUGHTON		MACLEAN
MACCOMBICH	STEWART OF APPIN	MACERRACHER	MACFARLANE	MACILREACH	MACDONALD
MACCOMBIE	THOMSON	MACFADZEAN	MACLAINE OF	MACILLERIACH	MACDONALD
MACCOMIE	THOMSON		LOCHBUIE	MACILRIACH	MACDONALD
MACCONACHER	MACDOUGALL	MACFALL	MACPHERSON	MACILREVIE	MACDONALD
MACCONACHIE	MACGREGOR,	MACFARQUHAR	FARQUHARSON	MACILVAIN	MACBEAN
	ROBERTSON	MACFATER	MACLAREN	MACILVORA	MACLAINE
MACCONCHY	MACKINTOSH	MACFEAT	MACLAREN		OF LOCHBUIE
MACCONDY	MACFARLANE	MACFERGUS	FERGUSSON	MACILVRAE	MACGILLIVRAY
MACCONNACH	MACKENZIE	MACGAW	MACFARLANE	MACILVRIDE	MACDONALD
MACCONNECHY	CAMPBELL,	MACGEACHIE	MACDONALD	MACILWHOM	LAMONT
	ROBERTSON		OF CLAN RANALD	MACILWRAITH	MACDONALD
MACCONNELL	MACDONALD	MACGEACHIN	MACDONALD	MACILZEGOWIE	LAMONT
MACCOOISH	MACDONALD		OF CLAN RANALD	MACIMMEY	FRASER
MACCORKHILL	GUNN	MACGEOCH	MACFARLANE	MACINALLY	BUCHANAN
MACCORKINDALE	MACLEOD	MACGHEE	MACKAY	MACINROY	ROBERTSON
MACCORKLE	GUNN	MACGHIE	MACKAY	MACINSTALKER	MACFARLANE
MACCORMACK	BUCHANAN	MACGILBERT	BUCHANAN	MACIOCK	MACFARLANE
MACCORMICK	MACLAINE OF	MACGILCHRIST	MACLACHLAN,	MACISSAC	CAMPBELL,
	LOCHBUIE		OGILVIE		MACDONALD
MACCORRIE	MACQUARRIE	MACGILL	MACDONALD	MACJAMES	MACFARLANE
MACCORRY	MACQUARRIE	MACGILLEDON	LAMONT	MACKAIL	CAMERON
MACCOSRAM	MACDONALD	MACGILLEGOWIE	LAMONT	MACKAMES	GUNN
MACCOULL	MACDOUGALL	MACGILLIVANTIC	MACDONALD	MACKASKILL	MACLEOD
MACCOWAN	COLQUHOUN,	MACGILLIVOUR	MACGILLIVRAY	MACKEACHAN	MACDONALD
	MACDOUGALL	MACGILLONIE	CAMERON	MACKEAMISH	GUNN,
MACCRAE	MACRAE	MACGILP	MACDONALD		MACDONALD
MACCRAIN	MACDONALD	MACGILROY	GRANT,	MACKECHNIE	MACDONALD
MACCRAKEN	MACLEAN		MACGILLIVRAY		OF CLAN RANALD
MACCRAW	MACRAE	MACGILVERNOCK	GRAHAM	MACKEE	MACKAY
MACCREATH	MACRAE	MACGILVRA	MACGILLIVRAY	MACKEGGIE	MACKINTOSH
MACCRIE	MACKAY	MACGORRIE	MACDONALD	MACKEITH	MACPHERSON
MACCRIMMOR	MACLEOD	MACGORRY	MACDONALD	MACKELLACHIE	MACDONALD

Surname	Clan	Surname	Clan	Surname	Clan
MACKELLAIGH	MACDONALD	MACLULICH	MACDOUGALL, MUNRO, ROSS	MACPHEIDIRAN	MACAULAY
MACKELLAR	CAMPBELL			MACPHILLIP	MACDONALD
MACKELLOCH	MACDONALD	MACLURE	MACLEOD	MACPHORICH	LAMONT
MACKELVIE	CAMPBELL	MACLYMONT	LAMONT	MACPHUN	MATHESON, CAMPBELL
MACKENDRICK	MACNAUGHTON	MACMANUS	COLQUHOUN, GUNN		
MACKENRICK	MACNAUGHTON			MACQUAIRE	MACQUARRIE
MACKEOCHAN	MACDONALD OF CLAN RANALD	MACMARTIN	CAMERON	MACQUEY	MACKAY
		MACMASTER	BUCHANAN, MACINNES	MACQUHIRR	MACQUARRIE
MACKERCHAR	FARQUHARSON			MACQUISTAN	MACDONALD
MACKERLICH	MACKENZIE	MACMATH	MATHESON	MACQUIRE	MACQUARRIE
MACKERRACHER	FARQUHARSON	MACMAURICE	BUCHANAN	MACQUOID	MAKAY
MACKERRAS	FERGUSSON	MACMENZIES	MENZIES	MACRA	MACRAE
MACKERSEY	FERGUSSON	MACMICHAEL	STEWART OF APPIN	MACRACH	MACRAE
MACKESSOCK	CAMPBELL, MACDONALD OF CLAN RANALD	MACMINN	MENZIES	MACRAILD	MACLEOD
		MACMONIES	MENZIES	MACRAITH	MACRAE, MACDONALD
MACKICHAN	MACDONALD OF CLAN RANALD, MACDOUGALL	MACMORRAN	MACKINNON		
		MACMUNN	STEWART	MACRANKIN	MACLEAN
		MACMURCHIE	BUCHANAN, MACKENZIE	MACRATH	MACRAE
MACKIESON	MACKINTOSH	MACMURCHY	BUCHANAN, MACKENZIE	MACROB	GUNN, MACFARLANE
MACKIGGAN	MACDONALD				
MACKILLIGAN	MACKINTOSH	MACMURDO	MACPHERSON	MACROBBIE	ROBERTSON, DRUMMOND
MACKILLOP	MACDONALD	MACMURDOCH	MACPHERSON	MACROBERT	ROBERTSON, DRUMMOND
MACKIM	FRASER	MACMURRAY	MURRAY		
MACKIMMIE	FRASER	MACMURRICH	MACDONALD OF CLAN RANALD, MACPHERSON	MACRORIE	MACDONALD
MACKINDLAY	FARQUHARSON			MACRORY	MACDONALD
MACKINLAY	BUCHANAN, FARQUHARSON, STEWART OF APPIN	MACMUTRIE	STEWART	MACRUER	MACDONALD
		MACNAIR	MACFARLANE, MACNAUGHTON	MACRURIE	MACDONALD
MACKINLEY	BUCHANAN			MACRURY	MACDONALD
MACKINNELL	MACDONALD	MACNAMELL	MACDOUGALL	MACSHANNACHAN	MACDONALD
MACKINNEY	MACKINNON	MACNAYER	MACNAUGHTON	MACSHIMES	FRASER OF LOVAT
MACKINNING	MACKINNON	MACNEE	MACGREGOR	MACSORLEY	CAMERON, MACDONALD
MACKINVEN	MACKINNON	MACNEILAGE	MACNEIL		
MACKIRDY	STEWART	MACNEILEDGE	MACNEIL	MACSPORRAN	MACDONALD
MACKISSOCK	CAMPBELL, MACDONALD OF CLAN RANALD	MACNEILLY	MACNEIL	MACSWAN	MACDONALD
		MACNEISH	MACGREGOR	MACSWEEN	MACDONALD
		MACNEUR	MACFARLANE	MACSWEN	MACDONALD
MACKNIGHT	MACNAUGHTON	MACNEY	MACGREGOR	MACSYMON	FRASER
MACLAE	STEWART OF APPIN	MACNIDER	MACFARLANE	MACTAGGART	ROSS
MACLAGAN	ROBERTSON	MACNIE	MACGREGOR	MACTARY	INNES
MACLAGHLAN	MACLACHLAN	MACNISH	MACGREGOR	MACTAUSE	CAMPBELL
MACLAIRISH	MACDONALD	MACNITER	MACFARLANE	MACTAVISH	CAMPBELL
MACLAMOND	LAMONT	MACNIVEN	CUMMING, MACKINTOSH, MACNAUGHTON	MACTEAR	ROSS, MACINTYRE
MACLARDIE	MACDONALD				
MACLARDY	MACDONALD			MACTIER	ROSS
MACLARTY	MACDONALD	MACNUIR	MACNAUGHTON	MACTIRE	ROSS
MACLAVERTY	MACDONALD	MACNUYER	BUCHANAN, MACNAUGHTON	MACULRIC	CAMERON
MACLAWS	CAMPBEL			MACURE	CAMPBELL
MACLEA	STEWART OF APPIN	MACOMIE	THOMSON	MACVAIL	CAMERON, MACKAY
MACLEAY	STEWART OF APPIN	MACOMISH	THOMSON		
MACLEHOSE	CAMPBELL	MACONIE	CAMERON	MACVANISH	MACKENZIE
MACLEISH	MACPHERSON	MACORAN	CAMPBELL	MACVARISH	MACDONALD OF CLAN RANALD
MACLEISTER	MACGREGOR	MACO'SHANNAIG	MACDONALD		
MACLERGAIN	MACLEAN	MACCOULL	MACDOUGALL	MACVEAGH	MACLEAN
MACLERIE	CAMERON, MACKINTOSH, MACPHERSON	MACCOURLIC	CAMERON	MACVEAN	MACBEAN
		MACOWEN	CAMPBELL	MACVEY	MACBEAN
		MACOWL	MACDOUGALL	MACVICAR	MACNAUGHTON
MACLEVERTY	MACDONALD	MACPATRICK	LAMONT, MACLAREN	MACVINISH	MACKENZIE
MACLEWIS	MACLEOD			MACVURICH	MACDONALD OF CLAN RANALD, MACPHERSON
MACLINTOCK	MACDOUGALL	MACPETRIE	MACGREGOR		
MACLISE	MACPHERSON	MACPHADDEN	MACLAINE OF LOCHBUIE	MACVURIE	MACDONALD OF CLAN RANALD
MACLIVER	MACGREGOR				
MACLUCAS	LAMONT, MACDOUGALL	MACPHATER	MACLAREN	MACWALRICK	CAMERON
		MACPHEDRAN	CAMPBELL	MACWALTER	MACFARLANE
MACLUGASH	MACDOUGALL	MACPHEDRON	MACAULAY	MACWATTIE	BUCHANAN

Surname	Clan	Surname	Clan	Surname	Clan
MACWHANNELL	MACDONALD	O'DRAIN	MACDONALD	SKINNER	MACGREGOR
MACWHIRR	MACQUARRIE	OLIVER	FRASER	SMALL	MURRAY
MACWHIRTER	BUCHANAN	O'MAY	SUTHERLAND	SMART	MACKENZIE
MACWILLIAM	GUNN,	O'SHAIG	MACDONALD	SMITH	MACPHERSON,
	MACFARLANE	O'SHANNACHAN	MACDONALD		MACKINTOSH
MALCOLMSON	MACCALLUM	O'SHANNAIG	MACDONALD	SORELY	CAMERON,
MALLOCH	MACGREGOR	PARK	MACDONALD		MACDONALD
MANN	GUNN	PARLANE	MACFARLANE	SPENCE	MACDUFF
MANSON	GUNN	PATON	MACDONALD,	SPITTAL	BUCHANAN
MARK	MACDONALD		MACLEAN	SPITTEL	BUCHANAN
MARNOCH	INNES	PATRICK	LAMONT	SPORRAN	MACDONALD
MARSHALL	KEITH	PAUL	CAMERON,	STALKER	MACFARLANE
MARTIN	CAMERON,		MACKINTOSH	STARK	ROBERTSON
	MACDONALD	PEARSON	MACPHERSON	STENHOUSE	BRUCE
MASON	SINCLAIR	PETERKIN	MACGREGOR	STORIE	OGILVIE
MASSEY	MATHESON	PETRIE	MACGREGOR	STRINGER	MACGREGOR
MASTERSON	BUCHANAN	PHILIPSON	MACDONALD	SUMMERS	LINDSAY
MATHIE	MATHESON	PINKERTON	CAMPBELL	SUTTIE	GRANT
MAVOR	GORDON	PIPER	MURRAY	SWAN	GUNN
MAY	MACDONALD	PITULLICH	MACDONALD	SWANSON	GUNN
MEANS	MENZIES	POLLARD	MACKAY	SYME	FRASER
MEILKEHAM	LAMONT	POLSON	MACKAY	SYMON	FRASER
MEIN	MENZIES	PORTER	MACNAUGHTON	TAGGART	ROSS
MENNIE	MENZIES	PRATT	GRANT	TARRILL	MACKINTOSH
MEYNERS	MENZIES	PURCELL	MACDONALD	TAWESSON	CAMPBELL
MICHIE	FORBES	RAITH	MACRAE	TAWSE	FARQUHARSON
MILLER	MACFARLANE	RANDOLF	BRUCE	THAIN	INNES,
MILNE	GORDON,	REIDFURD	INNES		MACKINTOSH
	OGILVIE	REOCH	FARQUHARSON,	TODD	GORDON
MILROY	MACGILLIVRAY		MACDONALD	TOLMIE	MACLEOD
MINN	MENZIES	REVIE	MACDONALD	TONNOCHY	ROBERTSON
MINNUS	MENZIES	RIACH	FARQUHARSON,	TORRY	CAMPBELL
MITCHELL	INNES		MACDONALD	TOSH	MACKINTOSH
MONACH	MACFARLANE	RICHARDSON	OGILVIE,	TOWARD	LAMONT
MONZIE	MENZIES		BUCHANAN	TOWART	LAMONT
MOODIE	STEWART	RISK	BUCHANAN	TRAIN	ROSS
MORAY	MURRAY	RITCHIE	MACKINTOSH	TURNER	LAMONT
MORGAN	MACKAY	ROBB	MACFARLANE	TYRE	MACINTYRE
MORREN	MACKINNON	ROBERTS	ROBERTSON	URE	CAMPBELL
MORRIS	BUCHANAN	ROBINSON	GUNN,	VASS	MUNRO,
MORTON	DOUGLAS		ROBERTSON		ROSS
MUNN	STEWART,	ROBISON	GUNN,	WALLIS	WALLACE
	LAMONT		ROBERTSON	WALTERS	FORBES
MURCHIE	BUCHANAN,	ROBSON	GUNN,	WASS	MUNRO,
	MENZIES		ROBERTSON		ROSS
MURCHISON	BUCHANAN,	ROME	JOHNSTONE	WATT	BUCHANAN
	MENZIES	RONALD	MACDONALD,	WEAVER	MACFARLANE
MURDOCH	MACDONALD,		GUNN	WEBSTER	MACFARLANE
	MACPHERSON	RONALDSON	MACDONALD,	WHANNELL	MACDONALD
MURDOSON	MACDONALD,		GUNN	WHARRIE	MACQUARRIE
	MACPHERSON	RORISON	MANDONALD	WHEELAN	MACDONALD
MURPHY	MACDONALD	ROY	ROBERTSON	WHITE	MACGREGOR,
NEAL	MACNEIL	RUSK	BUCHANAN		LAMONT
NEIL	MACNEIL	RUSKIN	BUCHANAN	WHYTE	MACGREGOR,
NEILL	MACNEIL	SANDERSON	MACDONALD		LAMONT
NEILSON	MACNEIL	SANDISON	GUNN	WILKIE	MACDONALD
NELSON	GUNN,	SAUNDERS	MACALISTER	WILKINSON	MACDONALD
	MACNEIL	SCOBIE	MACKAY	WILL	GUNN
NEISH	MACGREGOR	SHANNON	MACDONALD	WILLIAMSON	GUNN,
NISH	MACGREGOR	SHARP	STEWART		MACKAY
NIVEN	CUMMING,	SHERRY	MACKINNON	WILSON	GUNN, INNES
	MACKINTOSH	SIM	FRASER OF LOVAT	WRIGHT	MACINTYRE
NIXON	ARMSTRONG	SIME	FRASER OF LOVAT	WYLIE	GUNN,
NOBLE	MACKINTOSH	SIMON	FRASER OF LOVAT		MACFARLANE
NORIE	MACDONALD	SIMPSON	FRASER OF LOVAT	YUILL	BUCHANAN
NORMAN	SUTHERLAND	SIMSON	FRASER OF LOVAT	YULE	BUCHANAN

Kenneth I (MacAlpin)	843–860	Alexander II	1214–1249
Donald I	860–863	Alexander III	1249–1286
Constantine I	863–877	Margaret (Maid of Norway)	1286–1290
Aodh	877–878	First Interregnum	1290–1292
Eocha	878–889	John Balliol	1292–1296
Donald II	889–900	Second Interregnum	1296–1306
Constantine II	900–943	Robert I (the Bruce)	1306–1329
Malcolm I	943–954	David II	1329–1371
Indulph	954–962	Robert II (Stewart)	1371–1390
Dubh	962–967	Robert III	1390–1406
Culiean	967–971	James I	1406–1437
Kenneth II	971–995	James II	1437–1460
Constantine III	995–997	James III	1460–1488
Kenneth III	997–1005	James IV	1488–1513
Malcolm II	1005–1034	James V	1513–1542
Duncan I	1034–1040	Mary, Queen of Scots	1542–1567
MacBeth	1040–1057	James VI	1567–1625
Lulech	1057 (slain)	Charles I	1625–1649
Malcolm III (Canmore)	1057–1093	The Commonwealth & Protectorate	1651–1660
Donald Ban	1093 (deposed)	Charles I (crowned 1651, exiled and restored 1660)	1660–1685
Duncan II	1094 (slain)		
Donald Ban (restored)	1094–1097	James VII	1685–1688
Edgar	1097–1107	Mary II (with William II)	1689–1694
Alexander I	1107–1124	William II	1689–1702
David I	1124–1153	Anne	1702–1714
Malcolm IV (The Maiden)	1153–1165		
William I (The Lion)	1165–1214		

Index

Index

Acknowledgements

All tartans were supplied by Scottish Tartans Society. Heraldic crests were illustrated by Romilly Squire and supplied by kind permission of Harper Collins General Reference. The map on page 6 was drawn by Malcom Porter.

All photographs were supplied by the Still Moving Picture Company and the following photographers:-
Marius Alexander, page 19 right; M. Brooke, page 85; Clan Wallace, pages 18–19; Doug Corrance, pages 2, 9, 20–21, 49, 50–51, 56–57, 79, 91, 96–97, 100; Distant Images, pages 15 top, 34–35, 76–77; S. and N. Goodwin, pages 54–55, 88–89; Angus Johnston, pages 28–29, 30, 66–67; Derek Laird, pages 10–11, 24–25, 52; C. Patterson, page 37; Ken Patterson, pages 62, 64–65, 102; David Robertson, pages 4–5, 7, 27, 45, 48, 71, 72–73; S.T.B., pages 12 bottom, 15 bottom, 40–41, 42, 43, 53, 80, 82–83, 99; S.T.B./Paul Tomkins, pages 8, 12–13, 14, 18 left; Glyn Satterley, pages 32–33; David J. Whyte, page 68; Harvey Wood, pages 16–17, 46–47, 58–59, 94–95.